FAITH & WORD EDITION
BLEST ARE WE

Faith comes from what is heard,
and what is heard comes through the word of Christ.

Romans 10:17

Series Authors

Rev. Richard N. Fragomeni, Ph.D.
Maureen Gallagher, Ph.D.
Jeannine Goggin, M.P.S.
Michael P. Horan, Ph.D.

Scripture Co-editor and Consultant
Maria Pascuzzi, S.S.L., S.T.D.

Multicultural Consultant
Angela Erevia, M.C.D.P., M.R.E.

The Ad Hoc Committee to Oversee the Use of the Catechism, United States Conference of Catholic Bishops, has found this catechetical series, copyright 2008, to be in conformity with the Catechism of the Catholic Church.

This book reflects the
new revision of the

ROMAN
MISSAL
THIRD EDITION

Cincinnati, Ohio

FAITH & WORD EDITION
BLEST ARE WE®

Contributing Writers
Janie Gustafson, Ph.D.
Family Time Scripture: Michael J. Williams, M.S.
Feasts and Seasons: Marianne K. Lenihan
Our Catholic Heritage: Pat Enright

Advisory Board
William C. Allegri, M.A., Patricia M. Feeley, S.S.J., M.A., Edmund F. Gordon, Patricia A. Hoffmann, Cris V. Villapando, D.Min.

Consultants
Margaret J. Borders, M.R.S., Kelly O'Lague Dulka, M.S.W., Diane Hardick, M.A., Debra Schurko, Linda S. Tonelli, M.Ed., Joy Villotti-Biedrzycki

Music Advisor
GIA Publications: Michael A. Cymbala, Alec Harris, Robert W. Piercy

Nihil Obstat
M. Kathleen Flanagan, S.C., Ph.D.
Censor Librorum

Imprimatur
✠ Most Reverend Arthur J. Serratelli
Bishop of Paterson
April 25, 2006

The *nihil obstat* and *imprimatur* are official declarations that a book or pamphlet is free of doctrinal and moral error. No implication is contained therein that those who have granted the *nihil obstat* and *imprimatur* agree with the contents, opinions, or statements expressed.

Acknowledgments

Excerpts from the *New American Bible* with Revised New Testament and Psalms Copyright © 1991, 1986, 1970 Confraternity of Christian Doctrine, Inc., Washington, DC. Used with permission. All rights reserved. No portion of the *New American Bible* may be reprinted without permission in writing from the copyright holder.

All adaptions of Scripture are based on the *New American Bible* with Revised New Testament and Psalms Copyright © 1991, 1986, 1970 Confraternity of Christian Doctrine, Inc., Washington, DC.

Excerpts from the English translation of *Rite of Baptism for Children* © 1969, International Committee on English in the Liturgy, Inc. (ICEL); excerpts from the English translation of *The Roman Missal,* © 2010, ICEL. All rights reserved.

Excerpts from *Catholic Household Blessings and Prayers* (revised edition) © 2007, United States Conference of Catholic Bishops, Washington, D.C.

Music selections copyrighted and/or administered by GIA Publications are used with permission of GIA Publications, Inc., 7404 So Mason Avenue, Chicago, Illinois 60638-9927. Please refer to songs for specific copyright dates and information.

Arrangement of "Now Thank We All Our God," by Margaret W. Mealy, © 1981, GIA Publications, Inc. Used with permission.

In Appreciation: Blessed Kateri Church, Sparta, NJ; Church of the Assumption, Morristown, NJ; Our Lady of Mercy Church, Whippany, NJ; Our Lady of the Lake Church, Sparta, NJ; Saint Ann's Church, Parsippany, NJ; Saint Joseph's Church, Croton Falls, NY; Saint Peter the Apostle Church, Parsippany, NJ; Saint Thomas More Church, Convent Station, NJ; OCP Publications, Portland, OR; ILP Publications, Nashville, TN; GIA Publications, Inc., Chicago, IL; WLP Publications, Franklin Park, IL; Rev. George Hafemann

Credits
COVER: Gene Plaisted, OSC/The Crosiers

LET US PRAY ART: 9, 10, 11,12, 13 Jill Dubin; 14, 15 Teresa Flavin; 16 Beth Foster Wiggins

SCRIPTURE ART: Diane Paterson

ALL OTHER ART: 9–13, 34, 76, 79, 83, 88, 90, 98, 100, 102, 108, 110, 112, 131, 192, 198, 199, 236; Jill Dubin; 14–15 Teresa Flavin; 16, 75, 96 Beth Foster Wiggins; 17, 19, 24, 46, 48, 56, 58, 66, 68, 71, 120, 132, 140–144, 152, 154, 162, 166, 172, 174, 182, 184, 194, 196, 206, 212–216, 224, 226, 246-249 Diane Paterson; 18 Jaime Smith; 20 Elizabeth Wolf; 31, 64, 153 Lyn Martin; 31, 118, 243 Bernard Adnet; 33, 43, 54, 106, 157 Bernadette Lau; 35, 61 Tom Sperling; 37, 167, 176, 233, 240 Amanda Harvey; 50 Susan Gaber; 50, 82 Roman Dunets; 51, 138, 202 Nan Brooks; 53 Teresa Berasi; 57 Emily Thompson; 61 Ron Magnes; 69 Kristina Stephenson; 70 Pat Hoggan; 73 Laura Huliska-Beith; 73, 128, 239, 245 Anthony Lewis; 82 Winifred Barnum-Newman; 85, 117, 137, 170, 232 Dorothy Stott; 86 Reggie Holladay; 93, 253 Terra Muzick; 95 Shelley Dieterichs; 103 Gershom Griffith; 115 George Hamblin; 115, 135, 157 Patti Green; 121 Louise M. Baker; 130, 238 Heather Graham; 144, 148, 278 Cindy Rosenheim; 147 Jean & Mou-Sien Tseng; 160, 209 Gregg Valley; 187, 241 Morella Fuenmayor; 190, 233, 250, 253 Freddie Levin; 205 Jane Conteh Morgan; 219, 257 Randy Chewning; 234, 242, 255 Phyllis Pollema-Cahill; 237 Donna Perrone; 251 John Hovell

PHOTOS: Every effort has been made to secure permission and provide appropriate credit for photographic material. The publisher deeply regrets any omission and pledges to correct errors called to its attention in subsequent editions.

5 Myrleen Ferguson Cate/PhotoEdit; 6 Gene Plaisted/The Crosiers/Catholic News Service; 23 (Bkgd) Micha Bar'Am/©Magnum Photos , (Inset) Nancy Pierce/Black Star/PictureQuest; 36 Scibilia/Art Resource, NY; 40 Myrleen Ferguson Cate/PhotoEdit; 41 (TC, CL) James L. Shaffer; 42 ©Tom Till/Stone; 46 Art Resource, NY; 47 (TL) ©Elyse Lewin Studio Inc./Getty Images, (CR) J. Carini/Image Works, (BL) Jennie Woodcock/Corbis; 52 ©Gerrad Del Vecchio/Getty Images; 56 Photri, Inc.; 57 Jim Zuckerman/Corbis; 60 Myrleen Ferguson Cate/PhotoEdit; 62 Stephen Simpson/Getty Images; 65 (Bkgd) ©Sonia Halliday Photographs, (Bkgd) Bob Daemmrich/Stock Boston; 68 Neg. No. 323703, (Photo by John S. Nichols), Courtesy Dept. of Library Services/American Museum of Natural History; 74 ©Terry Donnelly; 78 SuperStock; 84 Tom Blagden/©Larry Ulrich Stock; 88 Erich Lessing/Art Resource, NY; 94 NRNPNX/Index Stock Imagery; 99 © Charles Gupton/Stock, Boston/PictureQuest; 104 Werner H. Muller/Peter Arnold, Inc.; 107 (Bkgd) Rene Burri/©Magnum Photos, (Inset) Jim Whitmer; 110 Erich Lessing/Art Resource, NY; 111 (L) Mary Kate Denny/PhotoEdit, ©John Terence Turner/Getty Images, (T) David Young-Wolff/PhotoEdit; 120 The Pierpont Morgan Library/Art Resource, NY; 122 SuperStock; 123 Myrleen Ferguson Cate/PhotoEdit; 124 (B, T) Saint Katharine Drexel Guild; 126 CP George/Visuals Unlimited; 130 Zev Radovan; 136 SuperStock; 141 (TR) Jim Whitmer, (CR) Robin RUdd/Unicorn Stock Photos, (B, CL) Myrleen Ferguson Cate/PhotoEdit; 146 SuperStock; 149 (Bkgd) Z. Radovan, Jerusalem, (Inset) Myrleen Cate/Photo Network/PictureQuest; 158 Robert Landau/Corbis; 162 Gene Plaisted, OSC/The Crosiers; 163 (B) ©George Kamper/Getty Images/Stone, (CL) Benjamin Fink/FoodPix, (R) David Young-Wolff/PhotoEdit; 164 Gene Plaisted/The Crosiers/Catholic News Service; 168 Erich Lessing/PhotoEdit; 172 Abegg-Stiftung, CH-3132 Riggisberg (Christop von Virag); 173 Bob Daemmrich/Image Works; 178 Tony Arruza/Corbis; 183 © Lynne Siler/Focus Group/PictureQuest; 186 Courtesy Mr. and Mrs. Edwin Pacheco; 188 Gene Plaisted, OSC/The Crosiers; 191 (Bkgd) Thomas Nebbia/NGS Image Collection, (Inset) Myrleen Ferguson Cate/PhotoEdit/PictureQuest; 193 Lawrence Migdale/Stock Boston; 194 P. Vauthey/Corbis Sygma; 195 (L) Laura Dwight/PhotoEdit, (R) Ellen Senisi/Image Works; 200 Erich Lessing/Art Resource, NY; 204 Sovfoto/Eastfoto; 210 Alfred B. Thomas/Animals Animals/Earth Scenes; 214 Marquette University Archives; 215 (BR) Antoine Gyori/Corbis, (CL) Brooks Kraft/Corbis Sygma, (TR) Christopher Morris/Black Star; 218 © Frank Fournier/Contact Press Images/PictureQuest; 220 Getty Images; 224 Brent Jones; 225 (L) Milt & Joan Mann/Cameramann International, Ltd., (R) PhotoDisc; 237 (T) ©Blend Images/Alamy, (B) Jeff Greenberg/AGE Fotostock; 244 Mryleen Ferguson Cate/PhotoEdit; 248 Skjold Photographs; 252 © Noah's Ark, 1978, Zeldis, Malcah (b.1931)/The Jewish Museum, NY/Art Resource, NY; 254 Luis Elvir/AP/Wide World; 256 Unterlinden Museum Colmar/Album/Joseph Martin/Art Archive; 258 (T) Tim Graham/Alamy Images, (B) © Alan Oddie/PhotoEdit; 259 (T) © Mary Kate Denny/Getty Images/Stone, (B) Skjold Photographs; 265 (C) Gene Plaisted, OSC/The Crosiers, (B) © W.P. Wittman; 266 (B) ©Masterfile Royalty-Free, (C) Gene Plaisted, OSC/The Crosiers, (BC) © W.P. Wittman; 271 Bob Daemmrich/Stock Boston; 273 © W.P. Wittman; 274 Alan Odie/PhotoEdit; 276 (T, B) Myrleen Cate/PhotoEdit; 277 (L) © Mary Kate Denny/Getty Images/Stone, (TR) Skjold Photographs, (BR) ©Myrleen Cate

S6001 ISBN 978-0-7829-1322-4

8th Printing. Manufactured for RCL Benziger in Cincinnati, OH, USA. January 2013.

CONTENTS

WHAT CATHOLICS BELIEVE

HOW CATHOLICS WORSHIP

HOW CATHOLICS LIVE

HOW CATHOLICS PRAY

FEASTS AND SEASONS

OUR CATHOLIC HERITAGE

Organized according to the 4 pillars of the Catechism

LET US PRAY

The Sign of the Cross

In the name of the Father,
and of the Son,
and of the Holy Spirit.
Amen.

Señal de la Cruz

En el nombre del Padre,
y del Hijo,
y del Espíritu Santo.
Amén.

The Lord's Prayer

Our Father, who art in heaven,
hallowed be thy name;
thy kingdom come,
thy will be done
on earth as it is in heaven.
Give us this day our daily bread,
and forgive us our trespasses,
as we forgive those who trespass
   against us;
and lead us not into temptation,
but deliver us from evil.

Amen.

The Hail Mary

Hail, Mary, full of grace,
the Lord is with thee.
Blessed art thou among women
and blessed is the fruit of thy
   womb, Jesus.
Holy Mary, Mother of God,
pray for us sinners,
now and at the hour of our death.
Amen.

Glory Be

Glory be to the Father
and to the Son
and to the Holy Spirit,
as it was in the beginning
is now, and ever shall be
world without end.
Amen.

Angel of God

A Prayer to My Guardian Angel

Angel of God, my guardian dear,
   to whom God's love commits me here,
ever this day be at my side,
   to light and guard, to rule and guide.
Amen.

Grace *Before* Meals

Bless us, O Lord,
    and these thy gifts,
    which we are about to
    receive from thy bounty,
    through Christ our Lord.
            Amen.

Grace *After* Meals

We give thanks,
    for all thy benefits,
    almighty God,
    who lives and reigns
    forever.
            Amen.

Morning Prayer

Loving God, bless the work we do.

Watch over us and guide us in school
and at home.

Help us realize that everything we do
gives praise to you.

We make this prayer in Jesus' name.

Amen.

Evening Prayer

Parent: May God bless you and keep you.

Child: May he guide you in life.

Parent: May he bless you
this evening.

Child: And keep us in
his sight.

Parent: May God be with
you, (name).

Child: And with your spirit.

Together: In the name of
the Father, and
of the Son, and
of the Holy Spirit.

Amen.

My Prayer

_____

- - - - - - - - - - - - - - - - - -

_____

- - - - - - - - - - - - - - - - - -

_____

- - - - - - - - - - - - - - - - - -

_____

- - - - - - - - - - - - - - - - - -

_____

- - - - - - - - - - - - - - - - - -

_____

- - - - - - - - - - - - - - - - - -

_____

AMEN.

The Bible

O God, we will listen to your words.

Based on Psalm 85:9

The Bible

The Bible is a special book about God.
It has two parts called the Old
Testament and the New Testament.
 The stories in the Old Testament
tell about God's love for his people
before Jesus was born.

The Story of Noah

The New Testament

The stories in the New Testament
tell about the life of Jesus and
his teachings.

You will learn more about the
Bible in Chapter 3.

Jesus Tells a Story

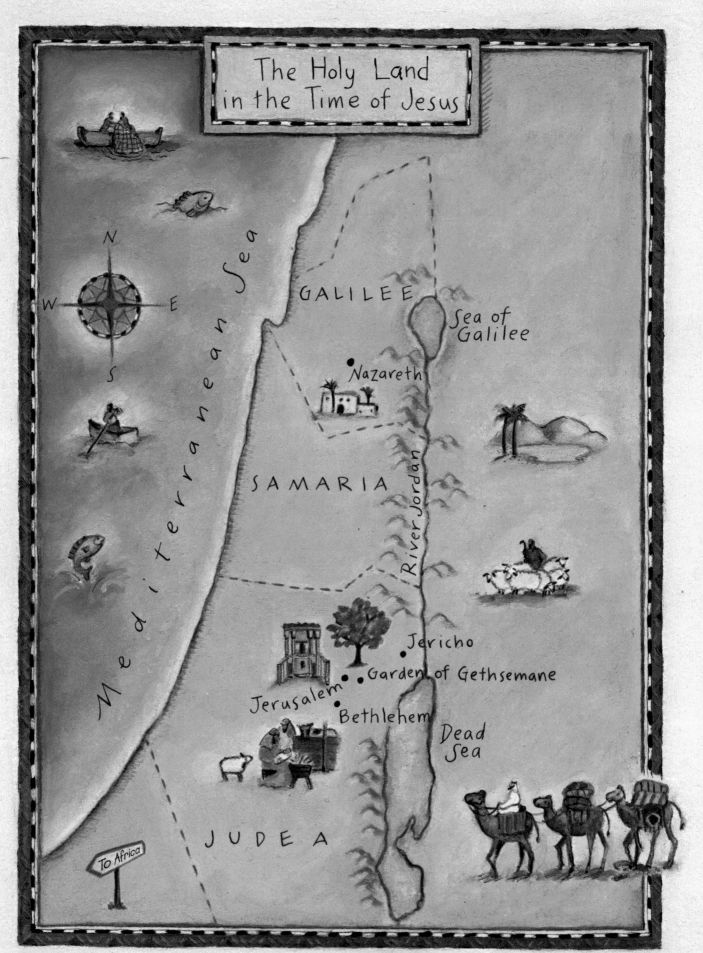

The Holy Land
in the Time of Jesus

Mediterranean Sea

GALILEE

Sea of
Galilee

Nazareth

SAMARIA

River Jordan

Jericho

Garden of Gethsemane

Jerusalem

Bethlehem

Dead
Sea

JUDEA

To Africa

N
W   E
S

The Map of the Holy Land

The Holy Land map shows places in the time of Jesus. It shows where he lived and worked. It shows where Jesus told people about God's love. You can read about these places in the Bible.

Activity

Remembering Bible Stories

Look at the pictures from the map. Circle each picture that reminds you of a Bible story. Tell about one of the stories you know.

1.

2.

3.

5.

4.

6.

BLEST ARE WE

Words and Music by David Haas
Spanish translation by Ronald F. Krisman

REFRAIN

Blest are we, ho-ly chil-dren of light are we!
¡Ben-de-ci-dos, so-mos san - tos hi-jos de la luz!

Blest are we, cho-sen peo-ple of God!
¡Ben-de-ci - dos y e - le-gi - dos por Dios!

Blest are we, God has plans for you and me!
¡Ben-de-ci - dos, Dios nos quie-re ser cual Je-sús!

Fine

Blest are we! We are the chil - dren of God!
¡Ben-de-ci - dos, so-mos los hi - jos de Dios!

VERSE

1. For our world, each sis - ter and broth - er:
1. *Por el mun - do, por to - dos sus pue - blos:*

We are called, called to serve!
¡So - mos lla - ma - dos pa - ra ser - vir!

We are here to love one an - oth - er:
Nos a - me - mos los u - nos a los o - tros;

D.C.

We are called, called to serve!
¡So - mos lla - ma - dos pa - ra ser - vir!

2. For the poor, the meek and the lowly:
   We are called, called to serve!
   For the weak, the sick and the hungry:
   We are called, called to serve!

3. For all those who yearn for freedom:
   We are called, called to serve!
   For the world, to be God's kingdom:
   We are called, called to serve!

2. *Por los pobres, los mansos y humildes:*
   ¡Somos llamados para servir!
   Por los enfermos, hambrientos, y débiles:
   ¡Somos llamados para servir!

3. *Por los que sufren y quieren ser librados:*
   ¡Somos llamados para servir!
   Venga a nosotros el Reino de los Cielos:
   ¡Somos llamados para servir!

Our Church Community

With our families, we belong to our parish church community. We come together to thank and praise God. We care for one another's needs.

I am the Good Shepherd. I know you by name. I care about you. You belong to me.

Based on John 10:14–15

Jesus cares for each of us just as the shepherd in the picture cares for his sheep. We follow Jesus when we care for people in our church community.

We Praise You

Words by Mike Balhoff

Music by Darryl Ducote and Gary Daigle

REFRAIN

We praise you, O Lord, for all your works are won-der-ful.

We praise you, O Lord, for ev-er is your love.

VERSE

1. Your wisdom made the heavens and the earth, O Lord;
   You formed the land then set the lights;
   And like your love the sun will rule the day,
   And stars will grace the night.

Take Home

FAMILY TIME

We Belong to Jesus' Church

In this first chapter, your child will learn that your family belongs to the community of Jesus' followers called the Catholic Church. From the Bible story of the Good Shepherd, your child will discover that Jesus calls us each by name to follow him. Finally, your child will learn to pray the Sign of the Cross as a sign of being Catholic.

ACTIVITY

Draw a Family Tree To help your child think about your extended family, draw a family tree and label the branches with the names of relatives you know, both living and deceased.

WEEKLY PLANNER

On Sunday

Notice that the Mass begins with the Sign of the Cross. It is a sign we share as Catholics, no matter what language we speak.

On the Web

www.blestarewe.com

Visit our Web site for the Saint of the day and the reflection question of the week.

Saint of The Week

 Saint Rose of Lima (1586–1617)

Rose grew up in a poor family in Peru. As a young woman, she cared for her parents. She set up a room in their home where poor children and the elderly could receive free health care. Rose of Lima became the first Saint of the Americas.

Feast Day: August 30

A Prayer for the Week

Loving God, bless our family as we begin this day. Help us follow the example of Saint Rose of Lima by loving and caring for others. Amen.

Take Home

FAMILY TIME

✝ Scripture Background

In the Time of Jesus

Shepherds In Palestine, shepherds cared for the most important domestic animal. The shepherd often walked miles guiding the flock to grass and water. He protected the sheep against attack from predators, often risking his own life. Each evening the shepherd led the flock back to the pen, counting to be sure that none were lost. He knew each sheep, and the sheep responded only to his voice. If even one were missing, the shepherd would go out and try to find it.

You can read Jesus' discourse about the good shepherd in John 10:1–21.

OUR CATHOLIC TRADITION in Art

Celtic Crosses There are many different crosses from different countries and different times in history. Stone crosses were erected in Ireland during the Viking invasion—a time of great destruction. The Irish needed a symbol of Christianity that would endure and that would tell stories from Scripture. Many of these Celtic crosses still stand today as a reminder to the Irish people of their strong Christian faith.

1 We Belong to Jesus' Church

 **I call you by name. You are mine.**

Based on Isaiah 43:1

Share

Everyone belongs to a family.

Families like doing things together.

Look at the picture. Tell about the families you see.

Draw your family at the picnic.

What other group do you belong to?

Hear & Believe

✝ Scripture The Good Shepherd

Shepherds take care of sheep. A good shepherd knows each sheep by name. The sheep come when they hear the shepherd's voice.

One day, Jesus said to his friends, "I am the Good Shepherd. I know you by name. I care for you. You belong to me."

Based on John 10:2–14

We Follow Jesus

Jesus is like a good shepherd. We are like the sheep. Jesus calls us by name. He loves us and cares for us. We follow Jesus.

Our Church Teaches

The **Catholic Church** is a community. A **community** is a group of people who belong together. Our church community is made up of people who follow Jesus. We love and care for others. We are called Catholics.

We Believe
The Church is the community of people who follow Jesus. Jesus calls us to follow him.

Faith Words
Catholic Church
The Catholic Church is the community of Jesus' followers. We belong to the Catholic Church.

What are some things Catholics do?

Respond

One Sunday Morning

One Sunday morning, Sam and his parents went to a new church. Some people smiled at them. Some said, "Hi."

"Why did those people smile at us?" Sam asked. "Why did they say, "Hi."

Sam's mother said, "We are all followers of Jesus. Our Church is like a big family. We care about each other."

Soon Sam had a smile on his face.

? Why do you think Sam began to smile?

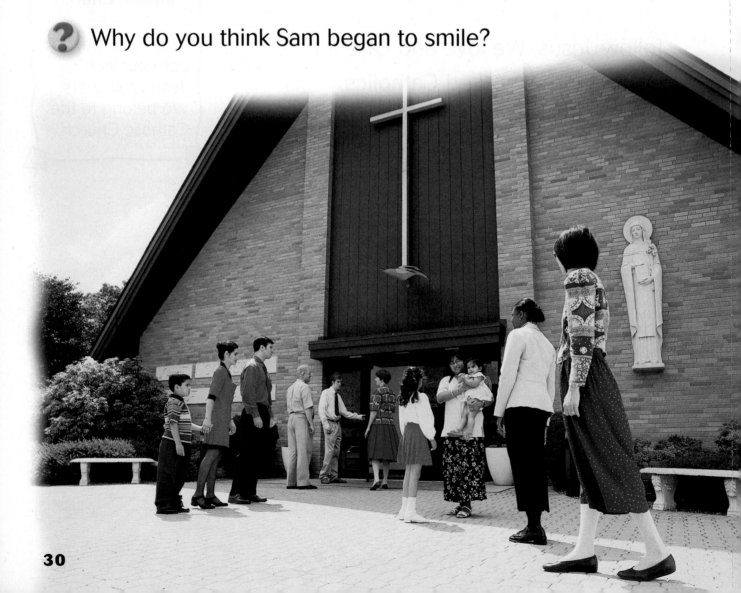

Activities

1. Tell how these people follow Jesus.
Draw a line from each picture to its word.

help

care

listen

pray

2. Write your first name here.

Jesus calls you by name

_____

- - - - - - - - - - - - - - - - -

_____

How can we
show that we
are Catholics?

Prayer Celebration

The Sign of the Cross

We use a special sign to show that we belong to the Catholic Church. Say the words and use your right hand to make the Sign of the Cross.

In the name of the Father

and of the Son

and of the Holy

Spirit.

Amen.

A **Circle** the word that best completes the sentence.

1. Jesus said, "I am the _____ Shepherd."
   Lost   **Good**

2. Jesus wants us to _____ others.
   love   **hurt**

3. People who belong to the Catholic Church follow _____.
   sheep   **Jesus**

4. We make the Sign of the Cross to show that we are _____.
   Catholic   **good**

B **Draw** one way you can follow Jesus.

Faith in Action

Caring and Sharing Our Lady of Mercy Parish has a "Caring and Sharing" group. The members help sick and hungry people. They help other people, too.

In Your Parish

Activity Imagine that a member of your parish is very sick. Draw a line from the car to the person's house. Look at the pictures along the way. Tell how your parish can help.

In Everyday Life

Activity Think of someone you know who needs help. What kind of help does this person need? How can you help?

Take Home

FAMILY TIME

We Gather to Celebrate Mass

In this chapter your child will learn that the church building is the place where the parish community gathers to celebrate Mass. Like your home, where family and friends come together on special occasions, your parish church is the place where your faith family gathers. Your child will learn that Jesus is present when members of your parish pray together. Some of the sacred objects found in church will also be presented.

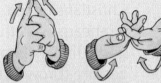

ACTIVITY

"Here's the Church..." Do you know the fingerplay, "Here's the church, here's the steeple, open the doors and see all the people"? If not, the illustrations may help you, or find someone to teach it to you. Then teach it to your child.

WEEKLY PLANNER

On Sunday

Arrive at church early. Notice how the area around the altar is decorated. See what is put on the altar as the priest celebrates Mass.

On the Web

www.blestarewe.com

 Visit our Web site for the Saint of the day and the reflection question of the week.

Saint of the Week

 Saint John Neumann (1811–1860)

John Neumann, born in Bohemia, came to America to become a priest. Father Neumann was first sent to work with German families near Buffalo, NY. Later, while serving as bishop of Philadelphia, ninety-eight Catholic schools and eighty new churches were built.

Feast Day: January 5

A Prayer for the Week

Lord God, we thank you for calling Saint John Neumann to build up the Church in America. Help us remember that when we gather to pray in our parish church, Jesus is with us. Amen.

FAMILY TIME

✝ Scripture Background

In the Time of Jesus and in Church History

The Sign of the Cross   Jesus commissioned his disciples with the words of the Sign of the Cross in Matthew 28:16–20. The gestures of the Sign of the Cross can be traced back to the second century A.D. Christians traced a small cross on their foreheads with their right thumb or a single finger. Two centuries later, the large gesture (brow to breast and shoulder to shoulder) was introduced, using two fingers representing the two natures of Christ. Before the end of the Middle Ages, the present form with open hand was common in the West.

OUR CATHOLIC TRADITION in Art

Stained-glass Windows   In the Middle Ages, Christians who could not read learned Bible stories from stained-glass windows. Scenes showing events from the life of Christ and stories of Saints were rendered in beautiful colored glass. The stained-glass window shown here is from Chartres Cathedral in France. It tells the story of Noah and the Flood.

Your church may have stained-glass windows, too. Check to see what stories are told in the windows of your church. If you're not certain what the stained-glass windows depict ask a member of your parish staff.

2 We Gather to Celebrate Mass

 **LET US PRAY**

When you gather in my name, I am with you.

Based on Matthew 18:20

Share

Catholics gather together in church.

Look at these churches.

How are they alike?

How are they different?

Circle the cross on each church. Then follow the dots to draw the cross in the middle of the page.

Why do we go to church?

Hear & Believe

Worship *We Gather Together*

Each week our Catholic community gathers in **church**. We gather to celebrate **Mass**.

We begin Mass with a song. Then the priest and the people pray these prayers.

Priest: In the name of the Father, and of the Son, and of the Holy Spirit.

People: Amen.

Priest: Grace to you and peace from God our Father and the Lord Jesus Christ.

People: And with your spirit.

The Order of Mass

The Beginning of Mass

The priest begins Mass with the Sign of the Cross. He says the words. We make the Sign of the Cross. We say, "Amen." Then the priest asks God to be with us. We ask God to be with the priest.

Our Church Teaches

Our Catholic community is called a **parish**. Jesus is with us when we gather in our parish church. He is with us when we pray. He is with us when our parish community gathers at Mass.

Faith Words

parish
A parish is a group of Catholics who belong to the same church community.

How can we take part in our parish?

Respond
Maria's Parish

Every Sunday, Maria and her family go to church. They belong to Saint Ann's Parish. Maria likes to sing and pray with her parish community. She likes to hear about ways her parish helps people. Maria is happy to belong to Saint Ann's Parish.

? What do you like about your parish?

Activity
Write the name of your parish church.

_____

- - - - - - - - - - - - - - - - - - -

_____

- - - - - - - - - - - - - - - - - - -

_____

Inside a Catholic Church

Parish churches look different on the outside. But they have many things the same on the inside. These things help us pray. They help us celebrate Mass. Here are some of the things in Maria's church.

altar

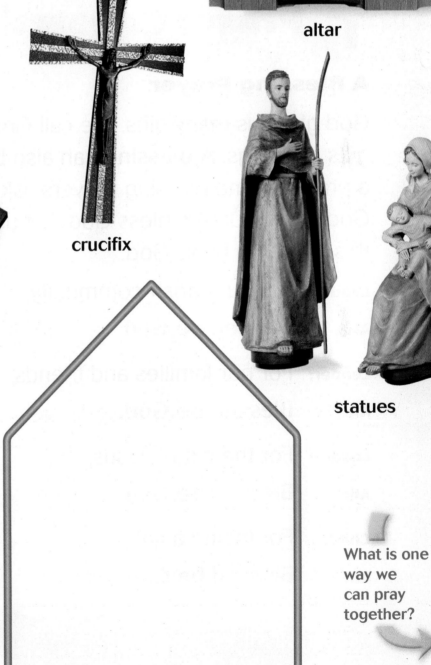

crucifix

statues

baptismal font

Activity

Draw something else that is in your church.

What is one way we can pray together?

Prayer Celebration

A Blessing Prayer

God gives us many gifts. We call God's gifts blessings. A **blessing** can also be a prayer. Some blessing prayers ask for God's care. Others bless God. Let us pray this prayer to bless God.

Leader: For our parish community,

All: Blessed be God.

Leader: For our families and friends,

All: Blessed be God.

Leader: For the gift of Jesus,

All: Blessed be God.

Child: For (name a gift),

All: Blessed be God.

Ⓐ Circle the words that best complete the sentences.

1. A group of Catholics who belong to the same church community is called a ____.

   parish   **school**

2. Catholics gather to celebrate Mass in a ____.

   store   **church**

3. When we gather to pray, ____ is with us.

   everyone   **Jesus**

4. A ____ prayer asks for God's care.

   blessing   **thank you**

Ⓑ Draw a line to match each word with its picture.

1. altar   ●   ●

2. crucifix   ●   ●

3. statue   ●   ●

4. baptismal font   ●   ●

5. church   ●   ●

Faith in Action

A Beautiful Church Many parishes have a group of people who decorate the church. In Advent they set up an Advent wreath. For Easter they use spring flowers and make joyful banners. The group makes their church look beautiful for each holy season.

In Everyday Life

Activity Close your eyes. Picture a room in your house. Think about one of the holy seasons. How could you decorate the room for this season? Tell about your ideas.

In Your Parish

Activity Decorate a church banner for Advent, Christmas, Lent, or Easter. Write the name of the holy season on your banner.

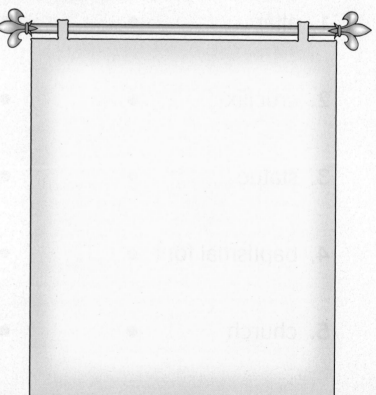

Take Home

FAMILY TIME

God's Word Teaches Us

This chapter teaches the children that the readings at Mass come from the Bible, the book that tells us about God's love and how to follow Jesus. The children will learn that God chose special people to write the Bible and that we call the Bible the "Word of God." They will hear about two men whose lives were changed by reading the Bible.

ACTIVITY

A Bible Story Picture Help your child draw a picture of a favorite Bible story and write a title for the drawing. Place the picture in a special place where your child will see it throughout the week.

WEEKLY PLANNER

On Sunday

Listen to the Gospel and the homily. At home, invite family members to tell what they would have said in the homily.

On the Web

www.blestarewe.com

Visit our Web site for the Saint of the day and the reflection question of the week.

Saint of The Week

Saint Augustine of Hippo (354–430)

Augustine lived with gusto, having a wild life and getting into much trouble. After reading God's Word in the Bible, he repented and became a fervent Christian. Augustine's writings defended the faith of the Church against heresy.

Patron Saint of: theologians
Feast Day: August 28

A Prayer for the Week

We thank you, Lord, for giving us the Bible. Help us learn how you want us to speak and act after hearing your holy Word. Amen.

Take Home

✠ Scripture Background

In the Time of the Early Church

Chariots   Chariots served two purposes in the history of Israel. The first was as attack vehicles, used in battle by King David and King Solomon. The second was as transportation for the rich and powerful. There was usually a separate driver who guided the chariot. The owner, often a member of the royal court, such as the Ethiopian in Chapter 3, might read or just enjoy the view. You can read about the conversion of the Ethiopian in Acts 8:26–40.

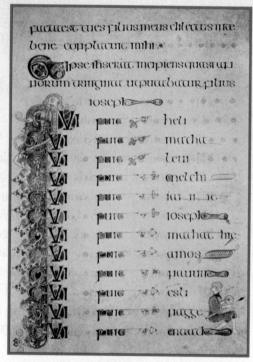

OUR CATHOLIC TRADITION in Art

Hand-copied Bibles   During the Middle Ages, monks from northern Africa, the Near East, and Europe made books by hand-copying every word. European monks became well known for copying the Bible many times. Painters, called illuminators, illustrated the Bibles using bright colors and lavish gold to create pictures called illuminations. These Bibles are treasures. They represent the monks' love for the Word of God. They are extraordinary works of art and holy keepsakes of our Catholic tradition.

Genealogy of Christ from *The Book of Kells*, Trinity College, Dublin, Ireland

3 God's Word Teaches Us

Hear God's word and keep it. Then you will be blessed.

Based on Luke 11:28

Share

We learn in many ways.
Look at the pictures.
Tell how each child learns.
Circle your favorite way
to learn.

How can
we learn
about God?

Hear & Believe

✝ Scripture A Man Learns About God

One day a man was on his way home to Africa. He was riding in a chariot. The man was reading his Bible. Philip saw the man and ran up to the chariot.

"Do you understand the Bible story?" Philip asked.

"No," the man said. "I need help."

Philip got into the chariot. He told the man about God's love. Philip told the man about Jesus.

The man from Africa became a follower of Jesus. He became a member of the Church.

Based on Acts 8:26–40

Learning About God

The man from Africa wanted to learn about God. Philip helped the man understand a story in the **Bible**. He helped the man become a follower of Jesus.

We listen to the Bible at Mass. The priest or deacon tells us about the Bible story. He helps us learn how to follow Jesus.

Our Church Teaches

The Bible is the Word of the God. God chose special people to write the Bible. Stories in the Bible teach us about God's love. They teach us how to love others. When we listen to the Word of God, we believe God speaks to us.

We Believe

God speaks to us through the Bible. The readings at Mass teach us about God's love and help us learn how to follow Jesus.

Faith Words
Bible
The Bible is the written Word of God. God chose special people to write the Bible.

How can we hear God's word?

Respond

Saint Augustine

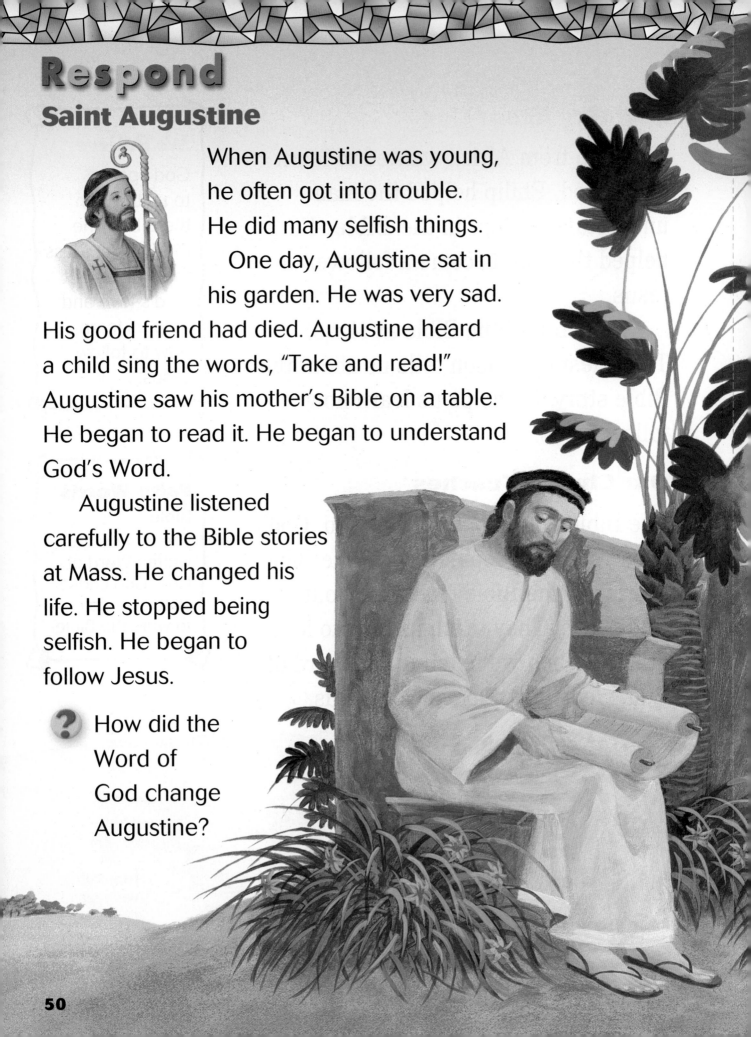

When Augustine was young, he often got into trouble. He did many selfish things.

One day, Augustine sat in his garden. He was very sad. His good friend had died. Augustine heard a child sing the words, "Take and read!" Augustine saw his mother's Bible on a table. He began to read it. He began to understand God's Word.

Augustine listened carefully to the Bible stories at Mass. He changed his life. He stopped being selfish. He began to follow Jesus.

? How did the Word of God change Augustine?

Activities

1. At Mass our parish community listens to God's Word. Draw yourself in the picture. Then draw your family and friends.

2. How can you hear God's Word?
   Trace the dotted letters to find out.

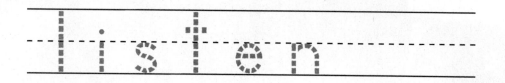

listen

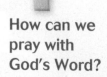

How can we pray with God's Word?

✝ Prayer Celebration

A Listening Prayer

Leader: O God, open our ears that we may hear.

All: Help us listen to your Word.

Leader: Listen to the Word of God.
Then think about what you hear.

Reader: Act as God's children. Obey your parents. Love others, just as Jesus did.

Based on Ephesians 5:1, 6:1

Reader (holds up Bible): The word of the Lord.

All: Thanks be to God.

(Pause)

Leader: O God, happy are we who hear your word and keep it.

All: O God, happy are we who hear your word and keep it.

Ⓐ Draw a line to connect the parts of each sentence.

God speaks to us through ●   ● Word of God

We hear the Word of God ●   ● the Bible

The Bible is the written ●   ● follow Jesus

Augustine read the Bible
and began to ●   ● at Mass

Ⓑ Draw or write about how you can learn about God.

Faith in Action

Priests and Deacons Men study for many years to become priests and deacons. They learn about the Bible. They learn about what our Church teaches. They learn how to help us follow Jesus.

In Your Parish

Activity Think about a Bible story that you listened to at Mass. What did the priest or deacon say about the story? Tell how what you learned can help you follow Jesus.

In Everyday Life

Activity Parts of our body help us learn. What parts can we use to learn about a Bible story?
Circle the picture that completes each sentence.

1. I hold the Bible with my ____.

2. I listen to God's Word with my ____.

3. I read a Bible story with my ____.

4. I think about a Bible story with my ____.

5. I tell others about God's Word with my ____.

Take Home

FAMILY TIME

We Give Praise to God

Learning how to praise God is the focus of this chapter. The children will learn that prayers of praise celebrate God's goodness. They will say, sing, and sign their praise to God. They will learn that the Gloria at Mass is a prayer of praise. They will also learn to pray with a psalm that praises God for his works of Creation.

ACTIVITY

Collect Family Symbols With your child, set up a display of objects that symbolizes the goodness or talents of your family. Possible examples include a cookbook, an artwork, and a sport's team photo. Make a sign that says, "Our Family Gives Praise."

WEEKLY PLANNER

On Sunday

At Mass, listen to the words of the Gloria. After Mass, name the expressions of praise that you heard.

On the Web

www.blestarewe.com

Visit our Web site for the Saint of the day and the reflection question of the week.

Saint of The Week

Saint Benedict Abbot (480–543)

Benedict, a student in Rome, left the city to live as a hermit. Recognizing his holiness, other men joined him. They lived a communal life that combined work and prayer. Benedict's rule required the monks to pray together seven times a day.

Feast Day: July 11

A Prayer for the Week

God our Father, we praise you for all your wonderful works. Help our family follow the example of Saint Benedict by making prayer an important part of our lives each day. Amen.

Take Home

FAMILY TIME

✝ Scripture Background

Before the Time of Jesus

Psalms In Hebrew, psalms are often called "praises." While these songs, or prayers, which make up what is often called the *Psalter* may have other themes, psalms are often personal hymns of praise to God for the marvels of his creation (Psalms 8, 148) and for his deeds for the people of Israel (Psalm 114). Other psalms of praise celebrate God as monarch (Psalms 96–99) or for his special dwelling in Zion (Psalms 46, 48, 76, 84, 87, 122). Try praising God by praying one or more of the psalms mentioned above.

OUR CATHOLIC TRADITION in Communications

Catacomb "Graffiti" Graffiti is something we usually think of as unsightly and messy. However, the early Christians in Rome created paintings and wrote messages of respect and remembrance in the form of blessings on the catacomb walls by the tombs of the martyrs. After a while, the "graffiti" became standardized. Messages from one Christian to another were sent in a code known only to other believers. Certain symbols were used over and over again, and have taken on meanings for all time.

4 We Give Praise to God

I will praise God with all my heart.

Based on Psalm 111:1

Share

We praise people when they do something good. We say, "Great job!"

Sometimes we praise a person just for being special. We say, "You are wonderful!"

Look at the picture. What do you think is happening?

Draw how your face looks when someone praises you.

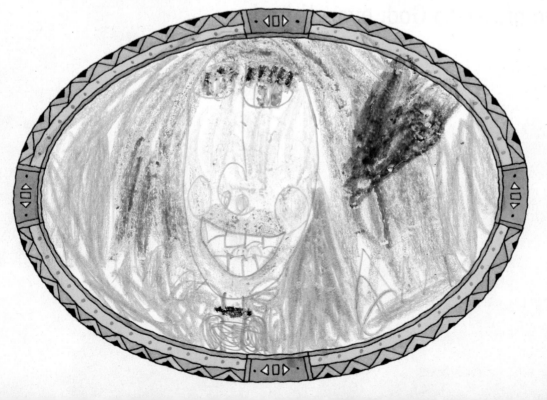

Why do we praise God?

Hear & Believe

✝ Scripture Praise God!

Everything that God makes
gives him praise.

Give praise to God, sun and moon.

Give praise to God, night and noon.

Give praise to God, mountains tall.

Give praise, people big and small.

Give praise to God, birds that sing.

Give praise to God, everything!

Based on Psalm 148

One Kind of Prayer

God is wonderful! God is good! Everything God made gives him **praise**. Praise is one kind of **prayer**. We praise God to celebrate his goodness.

Some prayers of praise are in the Bible. We can praise God anywhere. We can praise God any time.

Our Church Teaches

Prayer is listening to and talking to God. We can talk to God with prayers of praise. We can praise God with our parish community. We can tell God that he is good and wonderful.

How do Catholics praise God at Mass?

Respond

Glory to God

Joey learned about God even before he started school. He learned that God loves us. He learned that all good things come from God.

Now Joey is in the first grade. Each week he goes to Mass with his family. They praise God with their parish community. Sometimes they sing a prayer called the **Gloria**. Joey's favorite words are "Glory to God in the highest, and on earth peace to people of good will" (The Order of Mass).

? Why do you think Joey likes to sing the Gloria?

Activities

1. Learn to sign the words,
   "Sing praise to the Lord."

2. Read the words that praise God. Then use the numbers on the crayons to help you color the church window.

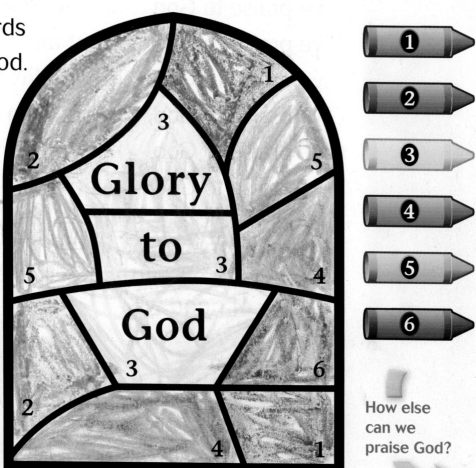

Glory to God

❶
❷
❸
❹
❺
❻

How else can we praise God?

Prayer Celebration

A Prayer of Praise

Leader: Everything God creates praises him.
Let us sign our praise to the Lord.

All (sign): Sing praise to the Lord.

Leader: Now let all creation praise God.

Side 1:	Side 2:
Give praise to God,	sun and moon.
Give praise to God,	night and noon.
Give praise to God,	mountains tall.
Give praise to God,	people big and small.
Give praise to God,	birds that sing.
Give praise to God,	everything.

Based on Psalm 148

All (sing): Glory to God in the highest,
and on earth peace to people
of good will.

A **Circle** the words that best complete the sentences.

1. Prayer is listening to and talking to ____.
   (God)   friends

2. We celebrate God's goodness with prayers of ____.
   sadness   (praise)

3. Some prayers of praise are in the ____.
   sun   (Bible)

4. Everything God made gives him ____.
   (power)   (praise)

5. We can praise God ____.
   (any time)   only at night

B **Complete** the prayer of praise that we sing at Mass. Write the number of the correct word in each box.

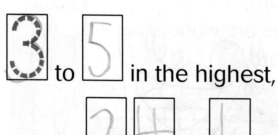

[3] to [5] in the highest,

and on [2][4] to [1] of good will.

1 people

3 Glory

2 earth

5 God

4 peace

Faith in Action

Children Sing to God   Some parishes have a children's choir. Boys and girls, small and tall, learn holy songs. They practice the songs many times. Then they sing the songs at Mass. The children praise God when they sing.

In Your Parish

Activity   Does your parish have a children's choir? Tell about the songs they sing. What is your favorite holy song? Tell why you like it.

In Everyday Life

Activity   Learn these words to the unit song, "We Praise You." Sing the words as a prayer. Then color the notes in the border.

We praise you, O Lord,
 for all your works are wonderful.
We praise you, O Lord,
 forever is your love.

Our Loving God

Jesus taught us that we are all God's special children.
God has given us the gift of his wonderful creation.
We thank God for all the gifts we have received.

Children, let us love one another.
Based on 1 John 4:7

Jesus went from town to town around the Sea of Galilee. He taught people about our loving God. When we show our love for others we follow Jesus.

Come All You People

Words and Music by Alexander Gondo
Arranged by John L. Bell

Come all you peo - ple, come and praise your Mak - er,

Come all you peo - ple, come and praise your Mak - er,

Come all you peo - ple, come and praise your Mak - er,

(Last time)

Come now and wor - ship the Lord.

Take Home

FAMILY TIME

God Is Our Loving Father

We look around us at all that God created and see signs of a loving Father. God not only gave us the gift of life, but continues to care for us. In this chapter the children will learn about God the Father's love for us and for all creation. They will discuss ways of caring for creation and will pray a prayer of thanks.

ACTIVITY

Pick a Card Remove the fours, threes, twos, and aces from a deck of cards. Shuffle the removed cards and put them face down on a table. Invite each family member to pick a card and to name different gifts from God. In other words, if a four is turned over, name four gifts; if an ace is turned over, name one gift.

WEEKLY PLANNER

On Sunday

At Mass we give thanks for all God's gifts. On the way to church, ask yourselves, "For what gifts are we thankful?"

On the Web

www.blestarewe.com

Visit our Web site for the Saint of the day and the reflection question of the week.

Saint of The Week

Saint Rose of Lima (1586–1617)

Rose grew up in a poor family in Peru. As a young woman, she cared for her parents. She set up a room in their home where poor children and the elderly could receive free health care. Rose of Lima became the first saint of the Americas.

Feast Day: August 30

A Prayer for the Week

Loving God, bless our family as we begin this day. Help us follow the example of Saint Rose of Lima by loving and caring for others. Amen.

Take Home

FAMILY TIME

Scripture Background

Before the Time of Jesus

Genesis and Creation Genesis, the first book of the Bible, tells the story of creation and of God's encounter with his first people. The Genesis account was not intended to be a scientific or historical account of creation. The authors of Genesis used the literary form of an allegory to reveal important truths about the nature of God. These truths include the preexistence of God, his wisdom and goodness, God's power through which all things are made, and the creation of man and woman in God's own image and likeness. The belief that God created everything good is repeated over and over again in Genesis.

You can read about creation in Genesis 1, 2.

Our Catholic Tradition in Science

Teilhard de Chardin Many people think there is a conflict between believing in the Bible and believing in evolution. They believe that if God created the world, then evolution could not have taken place. A French Jesuit priest in the early twentieth century tried to help us see God's hand in the scientific universe. Pierre Teilhard de Chardin believed that evolution was the ongoing work of God. He once wrote that he wanted to teach people how to see God everywhere, even in the most hidden places in the world.

5 God Is Our Loving Father

LET US PRAY O God, everything you made is wonderful!
Your love will last forever.

Based on Psalm 136:4

Share

God made all things.
All things show God's love.
Look at the picture.
Tell how each thing
shows God's love.

Draw something you like that
shows God's love.

Why did
God make
the world?

Hear & Believe

✝ Scripture God Creates The World

God made the  and ⬛ at night. God made the ☀ for warmth and light. And on the land, God planted 🌳, while in the sky flew 🕊 and 🐝. The 🌸 sprang up from the earth. Sweet 🍇 and 🍎 came to birth. The 🐟 and 🐊 swam in the seas. And on the land were 🐒. Soon 🐻 and 🐴 did appear, with 🐐 and 🐑, 🐑 and deer.

Based on Genesis 1:1–25

God Creates People

God saw that everything he made was good. Then God made people to be like himself. God told the people to take care of everything. He blessed the people and all that he had made.

Based on Genesis 1:26–31

Our Church Teaches

God is our loving Father. He wanted to **create** a beautiful world. God made the world out of nothing. God created everything in the world to show his love for us. God cares for us and for all creation. God is our **Creator**.

Faith Words

create
To create means "to make something out of nothing."

Creator
God is our Creator. God made everything in the world.

How can we care for God's creation?

Respond

Caring for Creation

Anna liked to play in her yard. She liked the little flower garden. Best of all, Anna liked the statue of Saint Francis. Anna learned that Francis loved everything God created. Francis took good care of plants. He was kind to animals. He helped people in need.

Anna picked up her watering can. She said, "Thank you, God, for making our world." Then Anna began to water the flowers.

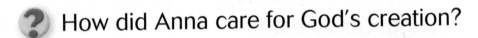 How did Anna care for God's creation?

Activities

1. Draw yourself in the heart. Think about how much God loves you.

God Loves Me.

God Made Me.

2. Here are some ways we care for God's creation. Draw a line from each way to its matching picture.

Help people in need.

Be kind to animals.

Share God's gifts.

How can we thank God for loving us?

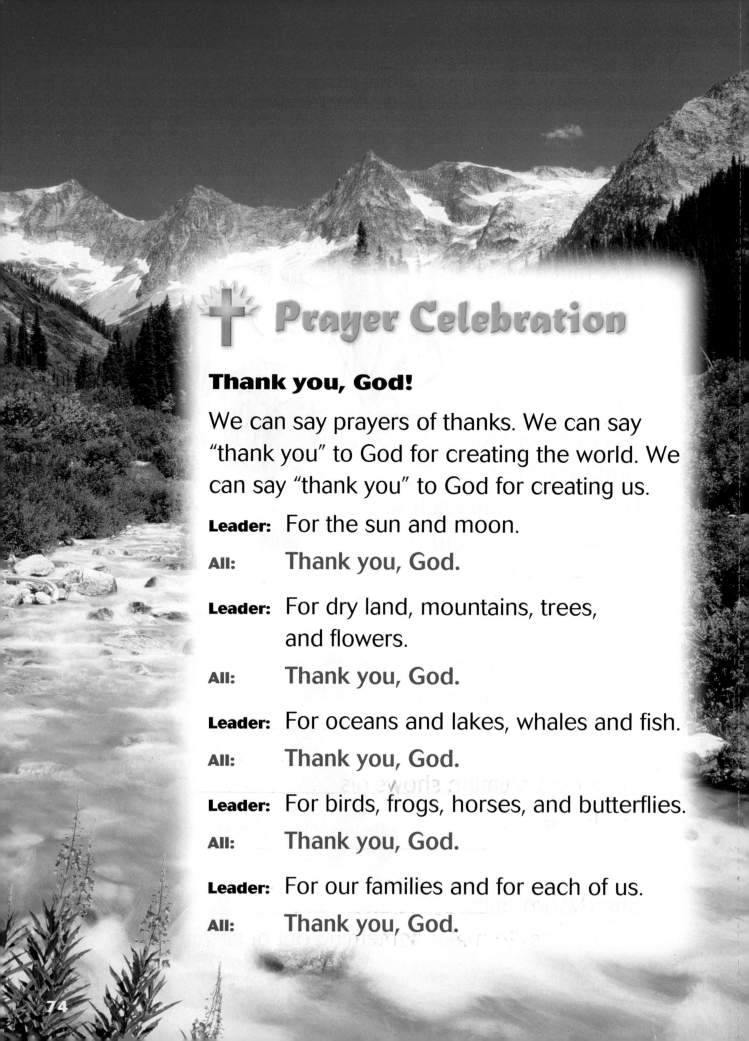

✝ Prayer Celebration

Thank you, God!

We can say prayers of thanks. We can say
"thank you" to God for creating the world. We
can say "thank you" to God for creating us.

Leader: For the sun and moon.

All: Thank you, God.

Leader: For dry land, mountains, trees,
and flowers.

All: Thank you, God.

Leader: For oceans and lakes, whales and fish.

All: Thank you, God.

Leader: For birds, frogs, horses, and butterflies.

All: Thank you, God.

Leader: For our families and for each of us.

All: Thank you, God.

A **Complete** the sentences with the words on the flowers.

1. Our loving Father and Creator is

_____ God _____ .

2. God made _____ people _____
to be like himself.

3. God's creation shows his _____ love _____
for us.

4. The word _____ create _____
means "to make something out of nothing."

Faith in Action

Caring for God's Creation   All Saints Parish invites its families to make the church grounds look beautiful. Some families plant flowers. Some water the plants. Others get rid of the weeds. The families who help show their love for God's creation.

In Your Parish

Activity   Picture the grounds around your parish church. What things that God created do you see? Tell how the families in your parish could care for God's creation.

In Everyday Life

Activity   Each day we make choices. Some choices help God's creation. Some choices hurt it. Circle the choices that help God's creation.

Take Home

FAMILY TIME

Baptism Is a Wonderful Gift

All Christians have received the wonderful gift of Baptism. This chapter discusses Baptism as a celebration of becoming a member of the Catholic Church and a follower of Jesus Christ. The children will learn that holy water is a sign of God's gift of new life. They will learn that God's loving presence in our lives is called grace.

ACTIVITY

Bless Your Child Bless your child with holy water by making a sign of the cross on his or her forehead while saying the words, "God be with you." Remind your child that God will always be there to help, and that your family will be there to listen and to give support.

WEEKLY PLANNER

On Sunday

Listen to the words of the Creed. This prayer states what we believe as Catholics. Discuss a belief from the Creed on the way home from church.

On the Web

www.blestarewe.com

Visit our Web site for the Saint of the day and the reflection question of the week.

Saint of the Week

Saint Kateri Tekakwitha (1656–1680)

Kateri Tekakwitha, a native American, was born in New York State. To be baptized demanded great courage, as her own people discriminated against her. Kateri escaped to Canada where she cared for the sick and taught Bible stories to children.

Feast Day: July 14

A Prayer for the Week

Lord, we thank you for the gift of Baptism. We are happy to be followers of Jesus. Help us share our faith with others by following the example of Saint Kateri Tekakwitha. Amen.

Take Home

† Scripture Background

In the Time of Jesus

Water Water played a vital role in the desert areas of Palestine. Always a symbol of life for humans, animals, and plants, water also served as an element of ritual purification before meals and in actions to effect cures for skin diseases or other ailments. The *Rite of Baptism* uses water to "cleanse" the soul of Original Sin, so that we may be "born of water and Spirit" (John 3:5), likening us to those whom God saved through the Flood.

You can read about Jesus' baptism by John in Mark 1:7–11 and Philip's baptism of the Ethiopian in Acts 8:36–38.

OUR CATHOLIC TRADITION in Art

Baptisteries Places where people are baptized are called *baptisteries*. In some churches they are very elaborate. Some baptisteries are separate from the church building itself and are richly decorated. One of the oldest baptisteries is in Rome at the Basilica of St. John Lateran. Construction began during the reign of Constantine in the fourth century. One of the most beautiful baptisteries stands opposite the Florence Cathedral in Italy. Legend has it that Michelangelo called its third pair of bronze doors, shown at right, "the Gates of Paradise."

6 Baptism Is a Wonderful Gift

 **LET US PRAY** The Church welcomes us with joy.
We belong to Jesus Christ.

Based on the Rite of Baptism

Share

We say "Welcome!" in many ways.
We put up signs. We bring gifts.
We shake hands. We share food.

Draw your own welcome picture.

How does
the Church
welcome us?

Hear & Believe

Worship Baptism Welcomes Us

The Church has a special celebration to welcome new members. We call the celebration Baptism.

The priest or deacon says, "The Christian community welcomes you with great joy."

During the celebration, the priest or deacon places the person in water three times. He says, "I baptize you in the name of the Father, and of the Son, and of the Holy Spirit."

Rite of Baptism

The Celebration of Baptism

In **Baptism** the priest or deacon places the person in holy water. Sometimes water is poured on the person's head three times. The water is a sign of God's gift of new life. Baptism is a sign that the new member belongs to the Catholic Church.

Our Church Teaches

In Baptism we become children of God. We become part of God's family. God shares his life with us. He shares his love with us. God's loving presence in our lives is called **grace**. God's gift of grace helps us follow Jesus. It helps us live as good Catholics.

How do Catholics follow Jesus?

Respond

Saint Kateri Tekakwitha

Kateri was a young Native American girl. A terrible sickness came to her village. Her parents died. The sickness left Kateri almost blind.

One day, a priest came. He told everyone about Jesus. Kateri wanted to be a follower of Jesus. She wanted to belong to the Church.

Kateri celebrated Baptism. She prayed to God every day. She helped people in need.

After Kateri died, many other Native Americans joined the Church. They wanted to live like Kateri and follow Jesus.

? Why did Kateri want to be baptized?

Activity

Circle the people who show us ways to follow Jesus.

How can we remember our Baptism?

83

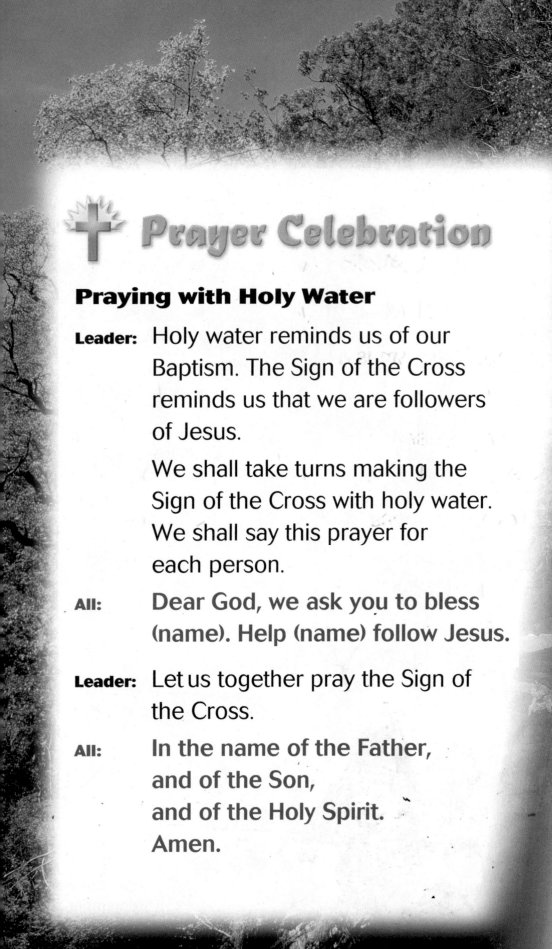

✝ Prayer Celebration

Praying with Holy Water

Leader: Holy water reminds us of our Baptism. The Sign of the Cross reminds us that we are followers of Jesus.

We shall take turns making the Sign of the Cross with holy water. We shall say this prayer for each person.

All: Dear God, we ask you to bless (name). Help (name) follow Jesus.

Leader: Let us together pray the Sign of the Cross.

All: In the name of the Father, and of the Son, and of the Holy Spirit. Amen.

A **Draw lines** to the words that complete the sentences.

1. In Baptism, we become members of the Catholic ● — ● welcome.

2. Baptism is a celebration of ● — ● life.

3. The water of Baptism is a sign of new ● — ● Church.

4. God's loving presence in our lives is called ● — ● baptized.

5. Kateri Tekakwitha was ● — ● grace.

B **Draw or write** about one way a Catholic can follow Jesus.

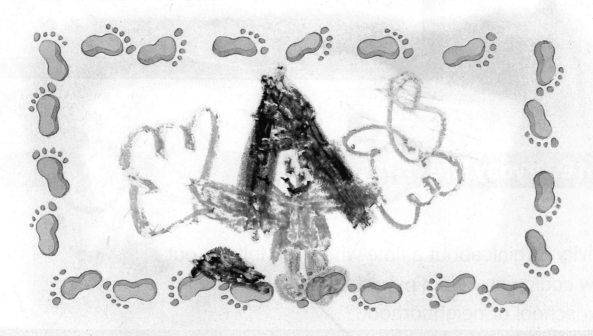

Faith in Action

Welcoming New Members Each month Saint Paul's Parish welcomes its new members. After Mass the welcome group serves coffee and snacks. Everyone gets to meet the new members. They talk about the parish. They talk about their families. They talk about helping others.

In Your Parish

Activity Make a welcome sign for your church. Draw pictures of people in your parish. Show how your parish is special.

Welcome

In Everyday Life

Activity Think about a time when you felt left out. How could you help a new child feel welcome in your school or neighborhood?

Take Home

FAMILY TIME

God Made Us to Be Good and Holy

In this chapter the children will learn that God made us to be loving people. By loving as Jesus did, we will recognize God's image in others and become holy. The children will also learn that God wants us to be happy with him forever in Heaven.

God is present in everyone.

Dad, Mom, me

Nana and Papa

My best friends

Snoopy

Aunt Carol

ACTIVITY

God's Presence Explain to your child that God made us and that he is present in each of us. Make a poster with the title, "God is present in everyone." Help your child paste photos or drawings of family members and friends onto the poster. Label the pictures.

WEEKLY PLANNER

On Sunday

God is present in everyone in your parish community. Introduce yourselves to someone you have not yet met before.

On the Web

www.blestarewe.com

Visit our Web site for the Saint of the day and the reflection question of the week.

Saint of the Week

Saint Elizabeth Ann Seton (1774–1821)

Elizabeth Seton, a wife and mother, felt God's call to become a Catholic after her husband died. She became a teacher and opened the first Catholic girls' school in the U.S. in Maryland. Elizabeth Seton founded the Sisters of Charity. In 1975 she became the first American born Saint.

Feast Day: January 4

A Prayer for the Week

Dear God, guide us along the path to heaven. Help us trust in you and show our love for others by following the example of Saint Elizabeth Ann Seton. Amen.

Take Home

FAMILY TIME

✝ Scripture Background

In the Time of Jesus

Scribes Scribes were Jewish men capable of reading and writing, who were experts in the law. They studied the Hebrew Scriptures, since they contained so much of the law of Israel. In the New Testament, scribes are often seen confronting Jesus on questions of the Mosaic Law. The scribe, or scholar of the law, in Luke's Gospel demonstrates his knowledge of the Book of Deuteronomy, where the Great Commandment is first found.

You can read about the Great Commandment in Luke 10:25–28 and in Deuteronomy 6:5.

OUR CATHOLIC TRADITION in Holy People

Saints Throughout history the Church has declared certain good and holy people Saints. Most Saints had ordinary lives before they became famous. They were dismissed or thought unusual by others for much of their lives. It was only after their deaths that their good works became known. Then the Church began the process that led to canonization.

All the Saints had one thing in common. They lived out the Great Commandment found in the Gospel of Luke, by loving God and loving their neighbor as themselves.

A tenth-century Byzantine ivory triptych of saints

7 God Made Us to Be Good and Holy

Children, let us love one another.

Based on 1 John 4:7

Share

Everything has a purpose.
Circle the things that you would
use in a playhouse.
Why did
you choose
each thing?

Draw one
more thing
to put in a
playhouse.

celses

Why did God
make us?

Hear & Believe

✝ Scripture A Man Questions Jesus

Jesus went from town to town teaching the people. One day, a man who knew God's law asked Jesus a question.

Man: What must I do to go to heaven?

Jesus (smiling): What is written in the Bible?

Man: Love God with your whole heart and with your whole mind. Love others as you love yourself.

Jesus: You are right. That is why God made you. That is what you must do to go to heaven.

Based on Luke 10:25–28

Why God Made Us

God created us to be like him. God made us to be good and **holy**. We are good and holy when we love God more than anything else. We are good and holy when we love ourselves. We are good and holy when we love other people. Jesus tells us that this is the way to **Heaven**.

Our Church Teaches

God created us to love him, ourselves, and other people. God made us to be happy with him forever in Heaven.

Someday every living thing will die. But death is not the end. If we love God and others, we will live forever. We will be with Jesus. We will be with all the good and holy people who ever lived. This will be the happiness of Heaven.

Faith Words

holy
To be holy means "to be like God."

Heaven
Heaven is happiness with God forever.

How can we show love for God and others?

Respond

A Man Named Peter

Peter could not think as fast as other people. He spoke very slowly. He walked with a limp. Some people made fun of Peter. But Peter always smiled back.

Peter liked people. He wanted to help them. That is why he liked his job at the grocery store. Peter packed the bags. Then he helped carry them out to the cars.

Peter listened to people's problems. He told the people that God loves them. Peter helped many people feel better.

When Peter died, people were very sad. They said, "Peter was a good and holy man. We were happy to know him."

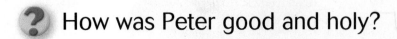 How was Peter good and holy?

Activity

Play the game about loving God and other people. Find your way to Jesus.

1. Each player needs a game marker.

2. Toss a penny.

3. Move 1 space for heads or 2 for tails.

You shared.
3
Go 1 more space.

4

You cared.
5
Go 1 more space.

2

You prayed.
1
Go 1 more space.

Start

6

You thanked God.
9
Go 1 more space.

8

You helped.
7
Go 1 more space.

Toss heads.
10
Go to Jesus.

Jesus

How can we celebrate being holy?

✝ Prayer Celebration

Praying with Movement

Prayer helps us know and love God. Moving our bodies can help us pray. The words and music of holy songs can help us move.

Let us move our bodies to the words and music of a holy song.

Write the number of the correct word in each box. The first one is done for you.

1. God made us to be 3 , and 2 .

2. To be holy is to be like 5 .

3. Jesus tells us to 1 God, ourselves, and other people.

4. If we do this, we will be 6 with God forever in 4 .

Faith in Action

Parish Greeters   On Sunday, members of Holy Family Parish greet people going into church. The greeters are friendly. They make the children feel special. Visitors always feel welcome.

In Your Parish

Activity   How do the greeters in your parish make you feel special? How can you help make your church a friendly place?

In Everyday Life

Activity   God loves you very much. He wants you to love yourself. Then you will be able to love others. Draw a picture of yourself. Then pray the prayer around your picture.

God, I know that you love me. Help me to love myself and other people.

Take Home

FAMILY TIME

We Give Thanks to God

God, our loving Father, gives us so much to be thankful for. In this chapter the children will identify some of God's special gifts. They will learn why we refer to God as "our Father," and that God's name is holy. They will experience thanking God with their hearts and with their voices.

OUR FAMILY

ACTIVITY

Thanksgiving A cornucopia, the horn-shaped basket filled with fruit and vegetables, represents the bounty we receive from the earth—from the goodness of the land God created. Tape a piece of construction paper in the shape of a cornucopia. Then fill it with fruit and vegetable shapes cut out of paper. Write something you and your child are thankful for on each shape.

WEEKLY PLANNER

On Sunday

The word *Eucharist* means "thanks," and the Mass is a prayer of thanksgiving. Have a thankful heart when you come to the liturgy this Sunday.

On the Web

www.blestarewe.com

Visit our Web site for the Saint of the day and the reflection question of the week.

Saint of the Week

 Saint Isidore the Farmer (1080–1130)

Isidore spent much of his life working on a farm in Spain. He and his wife Maria, also a Saint, showed their love for God by being kind to their neighbors. Although poor, Isidore and Maria shared their food with those poorer than themselves.

Patron Saint of: farmers and migrant workers
Feast Day: May 15

A Prayer for the Week

God our Father, we thank you for all your gifts. Help us follow the example of Saint Isidore by praying each day, by working hard, and by sharing our food with the poor. Amen.

Take Home

FAMILY TIME

✛ Scripture Background

In the Time of Jesus

Father In speaking of God the Father, Jesus used the Aramaic term "abba," which is a more intimate form of the word "father," much like "dad" would be in our language. This is probably why Christians began referring to God as "Father." Jesus teaches us to pray to God as "Our Father" because God represents the ideal loving and forgiving father who provides for his children and protects them from harm.

You can read about praying to God the Father in Matthew 6:6–15 and 7:7–11. Then slowly pray the Lord's Prayer.

OUR CATHOLIC TRADITION in Music

A Hymn of Thanks A well-known hymn of thanksgiving is "Now Thank We All Our God." The lyrics, based on Sirach 50:20–24, were originally written in German by Martin Rinkart under the title of "Nun danket alle Gott." The hymn probably first appeared in 1636. The hymn's composer, Johann Crüger, led the choir at St. Nicholas (Lutheran) Church in Berlin during the seventeenth century. He composed some of the finest hymn tunes of all times. Catherine Winkworth published the English translation of the hymn in 1858. Today "Now Thank We All Our God" is sung in many Catholic parishes on Thanksgiving Day.

8 We Give Thanks to God

Thank you, God, for your goodness.
We bless your name.

Based on Psalm 100:4

Share

Aunt Pat helped Nick
and Jenny bake cupcakes.
She said they could put
on the frosting. Nick and
Jenny surprised Aunt Pat.

Color the letters on
the cupcakes. How did
Nick and Jenny surprise
Aunt Pat?

Why does
God give
us gifts?

Hear & Believe

✝ Scripture God Is a Good Father

One day, Jesus told some people about God.

Jesus: God is like a good father. Imagine that you are a child. You are hungry. You ask your father for a loaf of bread. Will a good father give you a stone?

People: No!

Jesus: What will a good father give you?

People: A loaf of bread.

Jesus: That's right. Now pretend that you ask your father for a fish. Will a good father give you a snake?

People: No!

Jesus: What will a good father give you?

People: A fish.

Jesus: That's right. A good father knows how to give his children what they need. So too, God knows everything we need. God gives good gifts to everyone.

Based on Matthew 7:9–11

God Cares for Us

Jesus told the people that God is like a good father. God knows what everyone needs. He takes care of everyone. God wants us to pray for the things we need. Then God will give us what is good.

Our Church Teaches

Jesus taught us how to pray. He told us to call God "our Father." In the **Lord's Prayer** we say, "Our Father who art in heaven, **hallowed** be thy name." We tell God that his name is holy.

How do we show thanks for God's gifts?

Respond

The Man Who Said "Thank You"

One day, Jesus met ten people who had a sickness called leprosy. Jesus wanted to show the lepers that God loved them.

So Jesus said, "Go to the priests. Your sickness will go away."

All ten lepers did as Jesus said. Along the way, all ten got better. Their leprosy was gone! Nine of them ran off happy. But one man went back to Jesus.

"Thank you," the man said. "I will never forget this wonderful gift."

Then Jesus said, "Go, your faith has saved you."

Based on Luke 17:11–19

? Why was Jesus happy to see the man?

Activities

1. Trace the letters to complete the prayer.

Thank you, God,
for your gifts.
We bless your
holy name.

2. Draw one gift God has given you.

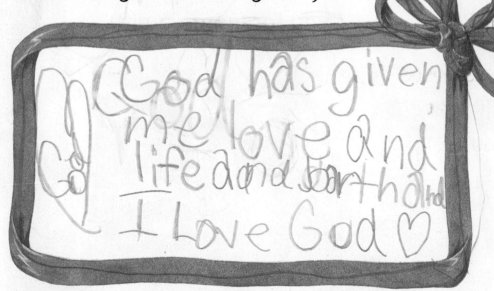

God has given
me love and
life and earth and
I Love God ♥

How can we say "thank you" to God?

✝ Prayer Celebration

A Thank You Prayer

Leader: We can say thank you to God with our hearts.
We can say thank you to God with our voices.
Let us thank God with our hearts and voices.

Reader 1: God, our Father, loves us in many ways. Let us thank God with our hearts. (Pause)

Reader 2: God, our Father, gives us many gifts. Let us thank God with our voices.

Each child: God, our Father, thank you for (name a gift).

A **Draw a line** to connect the parts of each sentence.

1. Jesus taught us to pray the ● ———— ● Lord's Prayer.

2. Hallowed means ● ● voices.

3. We pray the Lord's Prayer at ● ● Father.

4. We thank God with our hearts and ● ● Mass.

5. God is like a good ● ● holy.

B **Draw or write** about the leper who came back to see Jesus.

Faith in Action

Midnight Run   Some parishes collect food and clothes for homeless people in New York City. Homeless people do not have a home to sleep in. Many live on the street or in a park. During the year, members of the Midnight Run group drive into the city to give the food and clothes to the homeless.

In Your Parish

Activity   Circle the things that you think homeless people need. Draw a line under two things that you would like to give a homeless person.

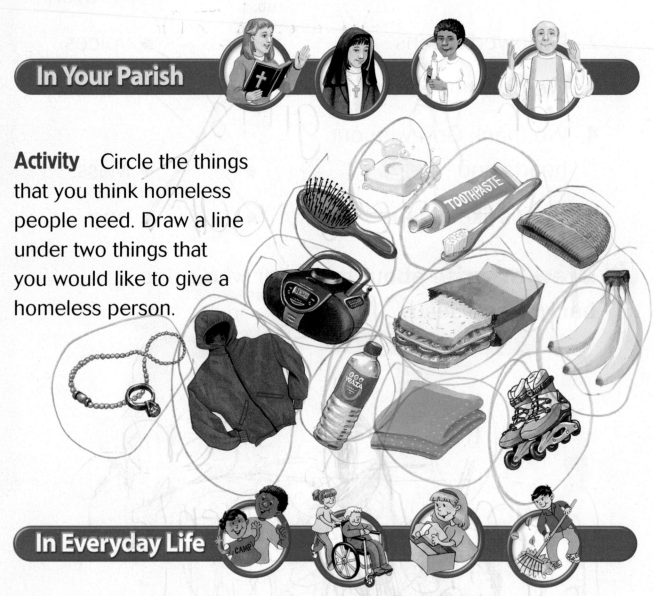

In Everyday Life

Activity   Close your eyes and picture the things that you have. As you see some of your favorite things, silently pray, "Thank you, God."

God's Son, Jesus

God's greatest gift to us is his Son, Jesus. Jesus showed us how to be a child of God. Jesus taught us how to care about one another.

Mary and her husband, Joseph, had to travel to the town of Bethlehem.

Based on Luke 2:1–7

Mary and Joseph traveled to Bethlehem on a road like this one. Jesus was born in Bethlehem. We can celebrate the birth of Jesus with prayer.

He Came Down

Traditional from Cameroon
Transcribed and Arranged by John L. Bell

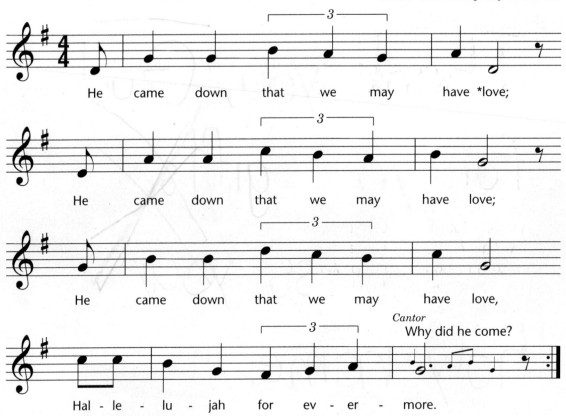

He came down that we may have *love;

He came down that we may have love;

He came down that we may have love,

Cantor
Why did he come?

Hal - le - lu - jah for ev - er - more.

*Substitute peace, joy, hope, life, etc.

Take Home

FAMILY TIME

Jesus Is God's Son

In this chapter the children will hear the Gospel story of the Annunciation. They will learn that the Angel Gabriel announced to Mary the Good News that she would be the mother of God's Son, Jesus. The children will also learn that God sent Jesus to be our Savior.

ACTIVITY

A "Good News" Collage Using old magazines, find and cut out pictures that show "good news." Arrange them on construction paper or poster board to make a collage. When it is finished, invite your child to tell about the good news in each picture.

WEEKLY PLANNER

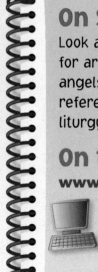

On Sunday

Look around your church for artwork depicting angels. Then listen for references to angels in the liturgy and in the hymns.

On the Web
www.blestarewe.com

Visit our Web site for the Saint of the day and the reflection question of the week.

Saint of the Week

Saint Joseph
(first century)

Joseph worked as a carpenter in Nazareth. He was chosen by God to be the husband of Mary and the foster father of Jesus. We know from the early events in Jesus' life that Joseph obeyed and trusted God and took good care of Jesus and Mary.

Patron Saint of: fathers and carpenters
Feast Days: March 19, May 1

A Prayer for the Week

Loving God, we are glad that you chose Joseph to care for Jesus and Mary. Help the members of our family love and care for one another as Jesus, Mary, and Joseph did. Amen.

Take Home

FAMILY TIME

✝ Scripture Background

In the Time of Jesus

Angels   Angels have always been seen as God's messengers to his human creation. In the Old Testament, God is seen as directly connecting with mankind on many occasions. However, over time, as God was looked upon as a being apart from the world, angels were seen as supernatural beings who acted as messengers to the world. They watched over God's people, and were sometimes instruments of God's justice. You can read about an angel announcing the birth of John the Baptist in Luke 1:11–20 and about the Angel Gabriel's visit to Mary in Luke 1:26–38.

OUR CATHOLIC TRADITION in Art

The Annunciation   The Annunciation is one of the most frequently depicted Scripture stories by famous "old master" artists. One of the greatest is by the Italian Renaissance master Fra Angelico (Brother Angel).

Brother Angel did many pictures, known as frescoes, on the walls of monks' rooms in his monastery in Florence, Italy. The Annunciation, however, he reserved for a very special place at the top of a staircase. The painting can still be seen in that same spot, just as it was hundreds of years ago.

9 Jesus Is God's Son

 We praise you, O God.
Your love for us is wonderful.

Based on Psalm 136:1–4

Share

Good news makes people happy.
Look at each picture.
Tell the good news that you
think each person hears.

Draw yourself hearing good news.

What Good
News did
God send?

Hear & Believe

✝ Scripture The Good News

A long time ago, God sent the Angel Gabriel to Mary. Gabriel had good news for Mary. He told Mary that God wanted her to be the mother of a special baby. God wanted her to name the baby Jesus. This special baby would be the Son of God. Mary said, "Yes, I will do whatever God wants."

Based on Luke 1:26–38

Mary Said Yes

Mary was a young Jewish woman who lived in Nazareth. She was good and holy. Mary listened to the **Angel** Gabriel's message. Mary said yes to God. She would be the mother of God's Son. Gabriel told Mary that God would watch over her. Mary trusted God.

Our Church Teaches

God loves us very much. God sent his own Son, **Jesus**, to be our **Savior**. Jesus was born in Bethlehem. Mary and her husband, **Joseph**, took care of him. Jesus shared his life with us and is always with us.

We Believe

God asked Mary to be the mother of his Son, Jesus. God sent Jesus to save us.

Faith Words

angel
An angel is a helper or messenger from God.

Savior
Jesus, the Son of God, is our Savior. He helps us and saves us.

How can we share the Good News about Jesus?

113

Respond

Telling the Good News

David likes his dad to read to him. He loves to hear Bible stories about Jesus. One day David's dad read about the birth of Jesus.

Later David went to play at his friend Mike's house. He told Mike the Good News about Jesus.

? What do you think David told his friend?

Activities

1. Learn to sign the words,
"I bring you the Good News."
Then share the Good News about
Jesus with others.

| I | bring | you | Good | News |

2. Color the spaces that have an **X** in them.
Whose name do you see?

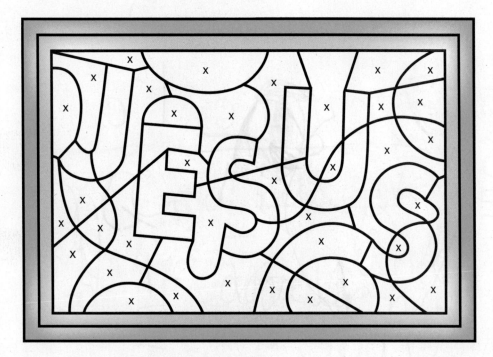

How can we
celebrate the
Good News
about Jesus?

Prayer Celebration

An Echo Prayer

Did you ever hear an echo?
You can pray an echo prayer.
Just repeat the words you hear.

Leader: Jesus, we believe you are the Son of God.

All: Jesus, we believe you are the Son of God.

Leader: Jesus, we believe you are always with us.

All: Jesus, we believe you are always with us.

Leader: Jesus, we believe you love us very much.

All: Jesus, we believe you love us very much.

A **Draw** a line to connect the parts of each sentence.

1. An angel is a   ●   ● own Son.

2. Mary said   ●   ● our Savior.

3. Jesus' mother is   ●   ● yes to God.

4. Jesus is God's   ●   ● Mary.

5. God sent Jesus to be   ●   ● messenger from God.

B **Write or draw** something that you can tell others about the Good News of Jesus' birth.

Faith in Action

Shawl Ministry Members of St. Francis de Sales Parish knit shawls for sick and lonely people. Each knitter prays for the person who will get the shawl. The shawls bring God's blessings of love and peace to many people.

In Your Parish

Activity How does your parish show that it cares for sick and lonely people? Write a note to a sick or lonely person. Tell the person that you will pray for him or her.

In Everyday Life

Activity We can love and care for people in many ways. How can you show your love to someone in your family? What can you do to make a friend feel special?

Take Home

FAMILY TIME

We Celebrate the Gift of Eucharist

In this chapter the children will come to recognize that the words of the Eucharistic Prayer at Mass describe the Last Supper that Jesus shared with his disciples on the night before he died. They will learn that Jesus is present in the Eucharist as a sign of God's love for us. During the prayer celebration the children will genuflect and bow as signs of respect for the Blessed Sacrament.

ACTIVITY

A Family Celebration Check your calendar to see when your next family celebration will be. Plan together for the event. Who will be invited? How will you decorate? What special foods will you have? Will you need help from family and friends?

WEEKLY PLANNER

On Sunday

Before Mass, make a visit to the tabernacle. Demonstrate how we genuflect and bow to show respect for the Blessed Sacrament.

On the Web

www.blestarewe.com

Visit our Web site for the Saint of the day and the reflection question of the week.

Saint of the Week

Saint Katharine Drexel (1858–1955)

Katharine Drexel founded the Sisters of the Blessed Sacrament. Their mission includes spreading the Gospel and teaching about the Eucharist. Katharine used her wealth to establish missions and schools for Native and African Americans. She was canonized a Saint in 2000 by Blessed Pope John Paul II.

Feast Day: March 3

A Prayer for the Week

Loving God, give us thankful hearts to celebrate the gift of your Son in the Eucharist. Help us share with others our belief that Jesus Christ is truly present in the Blessed Sacrament. Amen.

Take Home

FAMILY TIME

✝ Scripture Background

In the Time of Jesus

Passover Meal The Jewish Passover meal commemorated the freeing of the Israelites from Egypt, and comes from the passage, "I will pass over you; … no destructive blow will come upon you" (Exodus 12:13). Passover was and is the festival of freedom and redemption. Representative of God's love and saving acts, it always gave the people hope in the face of oppression to attain freedom from social discrimination and enjoy religious liberty. You can read accounts of Jesus' last Passover meal, the Last Supper, in Matthew 26:17–30, Mark 14:12–26, and Luke 22:7–20.

OUR CATHOLIC TRADITION in Worship

Tabernacles The word *tabernacle* means "tent," or "dwelling place." The word is used in the Bible to describe the special tent in which the Ark of the Covenant with the tablets of the law was kept while the Hebrew people were in the desert. When Solomon built the Temple in Jerusalem, the Ark was housed in the Holy of Holies. The place of the ark was considered God's presence on Earth.

In Catholic churches the tabernacle is the place where the Eucharist is reserved for those who cannot attend Mass. Catholics have the tradition of visiting the Blessed Sacrament in the tabernacle to pray and to remember that Jesus is present.

King David bringing the Ark of the Covenant into Jerusalem, shown in an illuminated manuscript by an unknown 14th–century artist

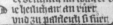

10 We Celebrate the Gift of Eucharist

 **LET US PRAY** When you eat this bread and drink from this cup of wine, remember me.

Based on Luke 22:19–20

Share

Special meals can be fun.

There is good food.

There are people we like.

Plan a special meal for your family.
Circle the foods you want at this meal.

Draw another food you would
like to eat at this meal.

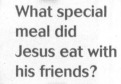

What special
meal did
Jesus eat with
his friends?

Hear & Believe

🕯️ Worship A Special Meal

On the night before he died, Jesus ate a special meal with his friends. We call this meal the Last Supper. Here is what Jesus said and did.

Jesus took bread from the table. He gave God thanks and praise. Then he broke the bread. He gave it to his friends and said, "Take this bread and eat of it, for this is my Body."

When supper was ended, Jesus took a cup of wine. He thanked God. He gave the cup to his friends and said, "Take this and drink from it. "This is the cup of my Blood."

Based on the Eucharistic Prayer, Roman Missal

Jesus Is with Us

At the **Last Supper**, Jesus shared the gift of himself with his friends. Today Jesus comes to us in the **Eucharist**. At Mass, we remember all that Jesus did and said at the Last Supper. After Mass, the Eucharist is kept in the **tabernacle** for the sick.

Our Church Teaches

Jesus **Christ** is present in the Eucharist. When we receive Holy Communion, we receive the Body and Blood of Jesus Christ. Christ is another name for Jesus. It reminds us that Jesus was sent by God to save all people.

Faith Words

Last Supper
The Last Supper is the special meal that Jesus shared with his friends. Jesus gave them the gift of himself.

Eucharist
The Eucharist is a special meal that Jesus shares with us today. We receive the Body and Blood of Jesus Christ.

How do we show our love for Christ in the Eucharist?

Respond

Saint Katharine Drexel

As a child, Katharine went to Mass with her family. She knew that the bread and wine are changed into the Body and Blood of Christ. Katharine learned that the Eucharist in the tabernacle is called the **Blessed Sacrament**.

Katharine's parents helped people in need. Katharine wanted to help, too.

When she grew up, Katharine helped Native Americans and African Americans. She paid to have schools built for them. Katharine started a community called the Sisters of the Blessed Sacrament. She and the sisters taught others about the Eucharist. They shared the Good News about Jesus.

St. Katharine Drexel by Brother Michael O'Neill McGrath, Bee Still Studios

? How did Katharine show her love for Jesus?

Activities

1. These objects help us remember Jesus.

   Connect the dots. What do you see?

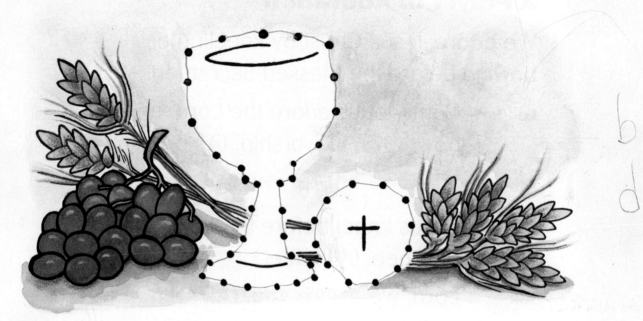

2. Do you remember what Jesus said
   at the Last Supper?

   Finish the sentences.

   Take this bread and eat of it, for this is my

   body

   Take this and drink from it.
   This is the cup of my

   blood

How can
we pray before
the Blessed
Sacrament?

Prayer Celebration

A Prayer of Adoration

We **adore** Jesus Christ by kneeling or bowing before the Blessed Sacrament.

Leader: Come let us adore the Lord, and bow down in worship. (All bow.)

All: Lord, we adore you. (All rise)

Leader: Let us kneel before the Lord on the left knee. (All kneel.)

All: Lord, we adore you. (All stand.)

Leader: Let us kneel before the Lord on the right knee. (All kneel.)

All: Lord, we adore you. (All stand.)

Leader: Let us kneel before the Lord on both knees. (All kneel.)

All: Lord, we adore you. (All stand.)

Based on Psalm 95:6–7 and the Maronite Rite of Kneeling

Complete the sentences with words from the box.

Jesus Christ	Sacrament	tabernacle
Last Supper	Body	

1. The _Last Supper_ is a
   special meal Jesus shared with his friends.

2. We believe _Jesus Christ_
   is present in the Eucharist.

3. Holy Communion for the sick is

   kept in the _Tabernacle_ .

4. Jesus said, "Take this bread and eat of it, for

   this is my _Body_ ."

5. Katharine Drexel started the Sisters of

   the Blessed _Sacrament_ .

Faith in Action

Special Helpers at Mass   Many people help a priest celebrate Mass. Some helpers give out Communion. The helpers say, "the Body of Christ" or "the Blood of Christ" to each person who comes to them. Each person answers, "Amen." These helpers are called extraordinary ministers of Holy Communion.

In Your Parish

Activity   Some special helpers bring the Eucharist to sick people. Use the code to complete the sentence below.

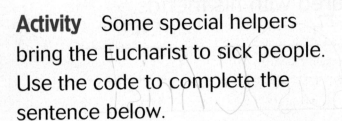

= A
= B
= C
= E
= L
= N
= R
= T

The Eucharist for sick people is kept in the

Tabernacle

In Everyday Life

Activity   Think about the meals you share with your family. How can you help make your family mealtime special?

Take Home

FAMILY TIME

Jesus Teaches Us About Forgiveness

In this chapter the children will hear the Bible story about Zacchaeus, a tax collector. They will learn that God's Laws help them make good choices. The children will come to understand the importance of saying they are sorry when they have chosen to do wrong. They will learn that God is always ready to forgive them.

ACTIVITY

Read All About It Read *Where the Wild Things Are* by Maurice Sendak (HarperCollins) with your child. Discuss the ending of the book as it relates to forgiveness and reconciliation.

WEEKLY PLANNER

On Sunday

Spend a few moments before Mass thinking about how you failed to be loving people. Pray, "Lord, have mercy," with reverence.

On the Web

www.blestarewe.com

Visit our Web site for the Saint of the day and the reflection question of the week.

Saint of the Week

 Saint John Vianney (1786–1859)

John Vianney was ordained a priest after the French Revolution, when the Church regained its freedom. He was sent to a poor parish in Ars where people were lax about their faith. Father Vianney prayed and fasted and the people began to return to church. They came from near and far to seek his advice.

Feast Day: August 4

A Prayer for the Week

Loving God, you are always ready to forgive us when we choose to do wrong. Help our family to be loving and forgiving in the days ahead. Amen.

Take Home

FAMILY TIME

✚ Scripture Background

In the Time of Jesus

Tax Collectors   Tax collectors, in the time of Jesus, were hated because they worked for the Romans, who were the occupiers of Palestine. Often, tax collectors overcharged their own people and could call upon Roman authority to punish those unwilling to pay the excessive rates. Jesus is accused of eating with sinners, when he goes to the homes of tax collectors named Matthew and Zacchaeus. Jesus even calls Matthew to be one of his Apostles.

You can read about these two men in Matthew 9:9–13 and Luke 19:1–10.

Our Catholic Tradition in Bible Times

Sycamore Trees   The Gospel story about Zacchaeus tells how he climbed up a sycamore tree to see Jesus over a crowd of people. The view from the sycamore tree enabled Zacchaeus, a short man, to see Jesus clearly.

Jericho, where the story takes place, is agriculturally rich and full of tree groves. The sycamore is a type of fig tree, called the mulberry fig, with edible fruit. This tree is not the same as the American sycamore. Zacchaeus found the Jericho tree convenient for climbing because of its low, spreading branches. Today, many families in Jericho still eat the figs from the sycamore tree.

11 Jesus Teaches Us about Forgiveness

Forgive me, O God, for I have done wrong.

Based on Luke 18:13

Share

Sometimes we do what is right.

Sometimes we do what is wrong.

Look at these pictures.

Draw a 😊 if the action is right.

Draw a 🙁 if the action is wrong.

What does Jesus teach us to do?

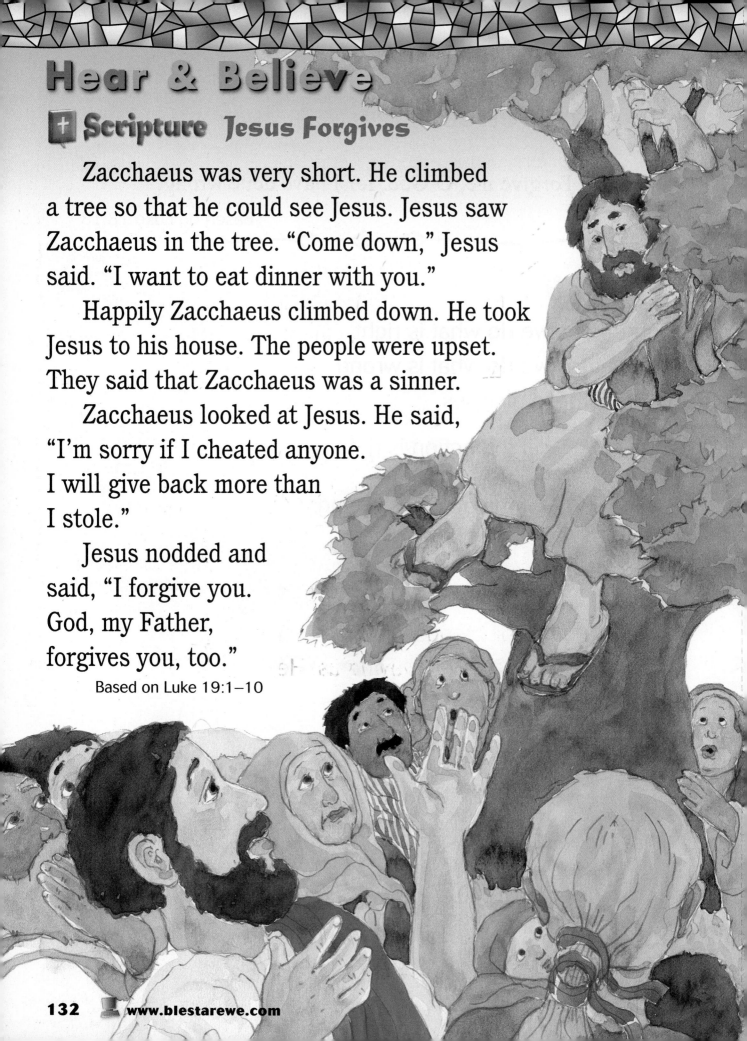

Hear & Believe

✝ Scripture Jesus Forgives

Zacchaeus was very short. He climbed a tree so that he could see Jesus. Jesus saw Zacchaeus in the tree. "Come down," Jesus said. "I want to eat dinner with you."

Happily Zacchaeus climbed down. He took Jesus to his house. The people were upset. They said that Zacchaeus was a sinner.

Zacchaeus looked at Jesus. He said, "I'm sorry if I cheated anyone. I will give back more than I stole."

Jesus nodded and said, "I forgive you. God, my Father, forgives you, too."

Based on Luke 19:1–10

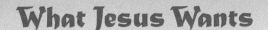

What Jesus Wants

Zacchaeus was a selfish man. But he was sorry and began to help others. Jesus loved Zacchaeus and forgave him. Jesus wants us to love God and others. When we do not act in a loving way, God wants us to be sorry. God will always **forgive** us.

Our Church Teaches

Jesus wants us to obey God's Laws. The Laws of God help us know and choose what is right. Sometimes we choose to do what is wrong. This is called **sin**. We turn away from God when we sin. Sin also hurts our friendship with other people. God never stops loving us. He is always ready to forgive us.

We Believe

God loves us and is always ready to forgive us. When we sin, God wants us to be sorry.

Faith Words
forgive
Forgive means "to excuse or to pardon."

sin
Sin is choosing to do something we know is wrong.

How can we be forgiven?

Respond

A Forgiveness Story

Ricky played his video game over and over again. His mom told him to stop. She told Ricky to do his homework. Ricky was angry and said something mean to his mom. So she sent him to his room.

Ricky lay on his bed. He heard his parents talking. He heard his little sisters playing. He wanted to be with them. But soon Ricky fell asleep.

When Ricky awoke, he saw a bowl of hot soup on his table. Next to the soup was a note from his mom.

? What do you think the note said?

Activities

1. Write the answers on the lines.

   If you hurt someone, what can you say?

   Sorry.

   Someone is sorry for hurting you. What can you say?

   I forgive you.

2. Color the spaces marked with a † green.

   Color the other spaces as you like.

   What words do you see?

How can we celebrate God's forgiveness?

135

Prayer Celebration

A Prayer for God's Mercy

At Mass we tell God we are sorry for our sins. Then we pray for God's **mercy**, or loving forgiveness.

Leader: Let us bow our heads and think about ways we have failed to love God and others. (Pause.)

Leader: For the times we have hurt others,

All: Lord, have mercy.

Leader: For the times we have not told the truth,

All: Christ, have mercy.

Leader: For the times we have not said, "I am sorry,"

All: Lord, have mercy.

A **Draw a line** to connect the parts of each sentence.

1. Jesus wants us to obey •   • loving us.

2. A choice to do something that we know is wrong is •   • forgive us.

3. Zacchaeus told Jesus that he was •   • God's Laws.

4. God never stops •   • a sin.

5. God is always ready to •   • sorry.

B **Write** the number of each picture before the words of the child who said them.

[3] "I forgive you."   [2] "I'm sorry, Mom."

[1] "Lord, have mercy."

1.   2.   3.

Faith in Action

Parish Workers   Each parish has workers who do important jobs. The secretary answers the phone, types the parish bulletin, and keeps the list of parish members up to date. The custodian cleans the church and makes sure the lights, heat, and air conditioner work. All parish workers should be respected and treated fairly.

In Your Parish

Activity   Who are some of the workers in your parish? What jobs do they do? How can your parish show respect for its workers?

In Everyday Life

Activity   People work to get the things they need for themselves and for their families.

People need food, water, a house, clothes, books, and a doctor's care.

Find and circle pictures of these needs.

Take Home

FAMILY TIME

We Pray with God's Word

In this chapter the children will discover how and where Jesus prayed. They will experience using their imagination to pray with the Gospel story of Jesus blessing the children. By putting themselves into the story, they will imagine what they would see, hear, feel, say, and do. The children will learn that praying with Bible stories can help them grow closer to Jesus.

ACTIVITY

Just Relax! To relax is the first step in praying with a Gospel story. Practice with your child. Sit comfortably in a quiet place. Close your eyes. Then breathe slowly while concentrating on your breathing. If you become distracted, bring your attention back to your breathing.

WEEKLY PLANNER

On Sunday

Listen carefully to the Gospel story during Mass. Imagine what it would be like to be in the story.

On the Web

www.blestarewe.com

 Visit our Web site for the Saint of the day and the reflection question of the week.

Saint of the Week

 Saint Mark **(first century)**

Mark traveled with Paul and Barnabas on their first missionary journey. Mark is one of the four Evangelists, or Gospel writers, and his was the first to be written. He wrote that Jesus understands our suffering and that we will one day share in Jesus' eternal glory.

Feast Day: April 25

 **A Prayer for the Week**

Dear Lord, bless our family with your presence. Help us hear your voice as we pray with Gospel stories. Help us live out the lessons we learn from your holy Word. Amen.

Take Home

FAMILY TIME

✝ Scripture Background

In the Time of Jesus

Children   Jesus blesses the children and tells his listeners that they must be like little children to enter the Kingdom of Heaven. The chief characteristic of children is acceptance; they know best how to accept gifts—with openness and faith. Jesus says that only those who accept the kingdom as a gift received through prayer and faith may enter it. Jesus goes against the common judgment of children in his day—that they hold no legal rights—by stating the special relationship they have with him. You can read about Jesus blessing the children in Mark 10:10–16.

OUR CATHOLIC TRADITION in Prayer

The Spiritual Exercises   Ignatius of Loyola, born in Spain in 1491, became the founder of the Jesuits. While studying his own spiritual life, Ignatius took notes on his experiences with prayer, suffering, and conversion of heart. His writings became known as the *Spiritual Exercises.* The exercises include Ignatius's approach to meditation. His method involves asking God for a special grace, reflecting on a Gospel scene by using one's imagination and senses, putting oneself into the scene, and applying the Gospel message to one's own life. Ignatius believed that everyone could learn to pray in this way. The *Spiritual Exercises* became Ignatius's greatest single contribution to Western spirituality.

12 We Pray with God's Word

 Lord, teach us how to pray.

Based on Luke 11:1

Share

People pray in many ways. Think about how you pray. How do you talk to and listen to God?

Mark an **X** in each picture that shows how you pray.

Circle your favorite way to pray.

How did Jesus pray?

Hear & Believe

✝ Scripture The Prayer of Jesus

The Bible tells us how and where Jesus prayed. He prayed with his heart and his voice. He prayed with his mind.

Jesus prayed with his family in the **Temple**. Jesus prayed alone in the desert. Sometimes he prayed on a mountain. Sometimes he prayed in a boat.

After the Last Supper, Jesus sang **psalms** with his friends. Then he went into a garden to pray.

The Temple in Jerusalem
Luke 2:41–52

A Bible land desert
Luke 4:1

A Bible land mountain
Matthew 14:23

Praying Like Jesus

We can learn to pray like Jesus.
We can pray aloud with our voices.
We can pray silently with our hearts
and minds. We can pray alone or with
other people. We can pray anywhere
and any time.

Our Church Teaches

We can pray with **Gospel** stories from
the Bible. The Gospels are the Good
News of Jesus. They tell us how to show
our love for God and other people.
We grow closer to Jesus when we pray
with the Gospels.

The Sea of Galilee

Matthew 14:13

The Garden of Gethsemane

Matthew 26:30

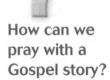

How can we pray with a Gospel story?

Respond

Praying with God's Word

There are four steps in praying with a Gospel story.

| Relax | Look and Listen | Imagine | Think |

Relax Close your eyes. Become quiet. Ask God to fill your heart and mind.

Look and Listen Look at the picture of Jesus and the children. Listen to the Bible story.

Jesus Blesses the Children

Jesus had been teaching all day. He was tired and sat down to rest.

Many parents started to bring their children to Jesus. They wanted Jesus to bless the children. But Jesus' friends told the people not to bother Jesus.

When Jesus saw this, he said, "Don't stop them. Let the children come closer. I love little children." Then Jesus placed his hands on the children. He gave them his blessing.

Based on Mark 10:13–16

Imagine Put yourself in the story. Imagine that your parents are taking you to see Jesus. He is on a hillside with his friends. Jesus is sitting under a tree.

Think Put yourself into the story. Ask yourself these questions.

Does Jesus see you?
Do you go up to him?
What do you say to Jesus?
What does Jesus say to you?

Activity

Draw yourself in the picture with Jesus and the children.

How else can we pray with a Gospel story?

✞ Prayer Celebration

An Acting Prayer

You can pray by acting out a Bible story. Putting on a play helps you to think about the story. You can imagine what the people said and did.

Act out the story of Jesus blessing the children.

A **Circle** the word that best completes each sentence.

1. Jesus prayed with his family in the ____.
   park   (Temple)

2. Prayers that we can sing are called ____.
   (psalms)   (Bibles)

3. The Gospel is the Good News of ____.
   Moses   (Jesus)

4. We can ____ with a Gospel story.
   (pray)   play

B **Think** about the Gospel story, "Jesus Blesses the Children." **Write** what you think Jesus said to one of the children.

you are good children and I god bless you

Faith in Action

Praying with Scripture   Each week in many parishes, small groups gather to pray. They read the Scripture readings for the next Sunday's Mass. They think about the readings. They share their thoughts. Then they pray about how they can show their love for God and others.

In Your Parish

Activity   Think of questions to ask your parish's prayer group. Plan to tell them how you pray with a Gospel story. Then you can be a teacher of prayer.

In Everyday Life

Activity   Choose and circle one of the places where Jesus prayed.

(desert)   (mountain)

garden   (boat)

Draw a picture of yourself praying with Jesus in that place.

In Bed

The Holy Spirit

J esus sends us the Holy Spirit to help us live as Jesus' followers. It is hard to know what God wants us to do. We can pray to the Holy Spirit for help.

Let us follow the Holy Spirit.
Based on Galatians 5:25

Paul sailed to different cities in a boat like this one. He taught people that the Holy Spirit is our helper. When we love others the Holy Spirit helps us to be kind.

If You Believe and I Believe

Traditional from Zimbabwe
Adaptation of English traditional as taught by Tarasai
Arranged by John L. Bell

If you be-lieve— and I be-lieve And we to-geth-er pray,—

The Ho - ly Spir - it must come down And set God's peo - ple free,—

And set God's peo - ple free,— And set God's peo - ple free;—

The Ho - ly Spir - it must come down And

set God's peo - ple free.—

Take Home

Jesus Promises the Holy Spirit

In this chapter the children will read about Jesus' promise to send the Holy Spirit. They will learn that the Holy Spirit is the gift of God's love. They will discover that the Holy Spirit helps us remember Jesus' teachings. Together they will praise God as Father, Son, and Holy Spirit.

ACTIVITY

A Welcome Sign   Showing a spirit of hospitality is one way to share love with others. Invite a family from your parish or neighborhood to your home for dinner or dessert. In preparation, discuss with your child the importance of hospitality, and together make a welcome sign for the family you invite.

WEEKLY PLANNER

On Sunday

One image of the Holy Spirit is the dove. Look for images of the Holy Spirit while you are at church.

On the Web

www.blestarewe.com

Visit our Web site for the Saint of the day and the reflection question of the week.

Saint of the Week

 Saint Dominic Savio (1842–1857)

Dominic Savio was born in Italy. At the time of his First Holy Communion, he considered Jesus and Mary to be his best friends. Dominic liked to pray and study, and was viewed as a peacemaker at his school. He became ill and died before his fifteenth birthday.

Patron Saint of: young boys
Feast Day: March 9

A Prayer for the Week

Come, Holy Spirit, fill our hearts with your gifts of love and peace. Help us follow the example of Saint Dominic Savio by being a sign of peace to everyone we meet. Amen.

Take Home

FAMILY TIME

✝ Scripture Background

In the Time of Jesus

The Advocate   In the Gospel of John 14:15–31, during the Last Supper discourses, Jesus makes a promise to his disciples. He says that after his departure, he will send another Advocate—himself being the first—to remain with them. Jesus specifies the conditions for receiving the Advocate as their love for him and the keeping of his Commandments. This Advocate is clearly the Holy Spirit, the Spirit of Truth, who after Jesus' Death and Resurrection will continue his work by helping the disciples understand the meaning of Jesus' teachings and deeds.

Our Catholic Tradition in Symbols

The Dove   The image of the dove representing the Holy Spirit goes back to the origins of the Church, and the image of the dove in Scripture goes back to the story of Noah. As a sign of the union of the Holy Spirit and Jesus, receptacles for the Eucharist were made in the shapes of doves, and hung in churches since the early Middle Ages. The Eucharist that was to be taken to the sick was in a container suspended by chains. The container was shaped like a dove and made of a precious metal, usually gold or silver. Later the dove was made of different materials, including gilded leather. The dove became the outer vessel holding the smaller container, or pyx, with the Blessed Sacrament inside.

13 Jesus Promises the Holy Spirit

 The Holy Spirit fills us with God's love.

Based on Romans 5:5

Share

Your family loves you very much.
Your family helps you in many ways.
But your family needs helpers to
care for you and to help you learn.

Tell how each person helps you.

Write about a person who helps you.

_____

- - - - - - - - - - - - - - - - - - - -

_____

_____

How does
Jesus
help us?

- - - - - - - - - - - - - - - - - - - -

_____

Hear & Believe

✝ Scripture A Special Helper

The friends of Jesus were sad. They did not want Jesus to leave them. "Stay with us," they begged.

Jesus shook his head. "I must go away, but I will not leave you alone. I will ask God, my Father, to send you the Holy Spirit."

"Who is the Holy Spirit?" they asked.

"The Holy Spirit is the helper my Father will send to those who love me," Jesus said. "The Holy Spirit will teach you more about God's love. The Holy Spirit will help you remember all that I have told you."

Jesus' friends looked worried.

"Don't be afraid," Jesus said. "The Holy Spirit will bring you peace. He will always be with you."

Based on John 14:15–31

Jesus' Promise

Jesus promised his friends that he would not leave them alone. He promised to send the **Holy Spirit** to be their helper. The Holy Spirit is our helper, too. The Holy Spirit helps us follow Jesus. He helps us love others. The Holy Spirit brings us peace.

Our Church Teaches

God the Holy Spirit is the gift of God's love to us. The Holy Spirit is always with us. He helps us and guides us.

We Believe

The Holy Spirit is always with us. The Holy Spirit helps us and guides us.

Faith Words

Holy Spirit
The Holy Spirit is God. The Holy Spirit helps us follow Jesus.

How else can the Holy Spirit help us?

Respond

Terry's Problem

One morning, Terry was waiting for the school bus. Something very scary happened. Two older boys pushed a first grade boy into the street. The older boys thought it was funny. They began to laugh.

When Terry got to school, she told her teacher what happened. Terry was afraid that the other children might tease her.

That night, Terry's mother said, "You did the right thing. Your teacher will know how to handle the problem."

At bedtime Terry's mother taught her this prayer. "Holy Spirit, help me always do what is right."

? Why did Terry's mother teach her this prayer?

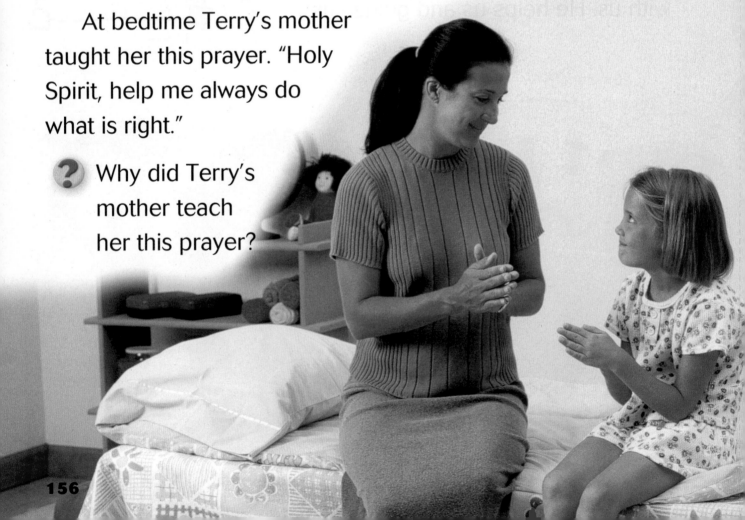

Activities

1. Color the border around the prayer. Then pray the prayer.

Holy Spirit, help me always do what is right.

2. Draw about a time when you could ask the Holy Spirit for help.

How can we celebrate God's gift of the Holy Spirit?

Prayer Celebration

Glory Be

We praise God as Father, Son, and Holy Spirit when we make the Sign of the Cross. Let us now praise God by praying the Glory Be.

Glory be to the Father
and to the Son
and to the Holy Spirit,
as it was in the beginning
is now, and ever shall be
world without end.   Amen.

A **Draw** lines to the words that complete the sentences.

1. Jesus promised to send ● ● helper.

2. The Holy Spirit helps us ● ● God's love.

3. The Holy Spirit is our ● ● the Holy Spirit.

4. The Holy Spirit is a gift of ● ● with us.

5. The Holy Spirit is always ● ● follow Jesus.

B **Circle** the words that name choices the Holy Spirit helps people make.

1. Susan will _____ at home.
   help   **be lazy**

2. José will _____ when he plays with his friends.
   cheat   **be fair**

3. Kim will _____ at Mass.
   play   **pray**

4. David will _____ at school.
   listen   **not listen**

Faith in Action

Catechists   Some men and women become catechists. They share their faith with others. Catechists teach children about God. The children learn Bible stories. They learn how to follow Jesus. The Holy Spirit guides catechists in their work.

In Your Parish

Activity   You can ask the Holy Spirit to help your catechist. Learn this prayer. Color the border. Then pray for your catechist.

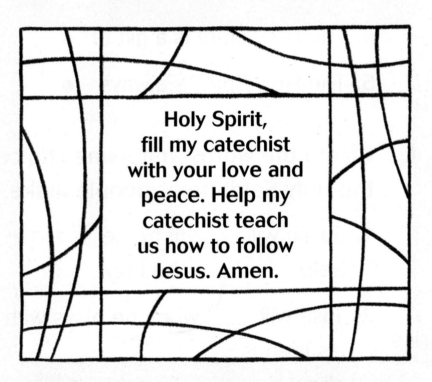

Holy Spirit, fill my catechist with your love and peace. Help my catechist teach us how to follow Jesus. Amen.

In Everyday Life

Activity   The Holy Spirit helps us share our faith with others. What could you tell someone in your family about Jesus? What could you tell a friend about the Mass?

Take Home

FAMILY TIME

We Celebrate the Gift of the Holy Spirit

In this chapter the children will learn that they receive God's gift of the Holy Spirit in the Sacraments. They will learn that the pouring of water in Baptism is a sign that all sin is washed away and that we are filled with God's love. The children will also learn that the oil used in Confirmation is a sign that the Holy Spirit is working in us to make our faith stronger.

ACTIVITY

Remembering Baptism Locate your child's baptismal certificate. Together, find the date and place of your child's Baptism. Talk about this special day. Plan a family celebration. If possible, invite your child's godparents.

WEEKLY PLANNER

On Sunday

Look at the baptismal font in your church. Remind your family that the Holy Spirit first came to them at Baptism.

On the Web

www.blestarewe.com

 Visit our Web site for the Saint of the day and the reflection question of the week.

Saint of the Week

 Saint Turibius (1538–1606)

Turibius, a judge in Spain, was appointed archbishop of Lima, Peru in 1580. He visited the villages in his territory, baptizing and confirming the people. Bishop Turibius built hospitals and became an advocate for the poor. He died during his last missionary journey.

Patron Saint of: Latin American bishops
Feast Day: March 23

A Prayer for the Week

Spirit of God, at our Baptism we were called to follow Jesus. Guide us as we try to follow the example of Saint Turibius. Help us spread the Good News and share our gifts with the poor. Amen.

Take Home

FAMILY TIME

✝ Scripture Background

In the Time of Jesus

Nicodemus Nicodemus was a Pharisee, a teacher, and a leader of the Jews. He appears in John's Gospel three times: questioning Jesus (John 3:1–21); defending Jesus (John 7:50–52); preparing Jesus' body for burial with Joseph of Arimathea (John 19:39). He seems to personify certain learned Jews who were well disposed toward Jesus, but did not adequately understand him, and had not reached the point of accepting him publicly. You may wish to read about Nicodemus questioning Jesus in John 3:1–21.

OUR CATHOLIC TRADITION in Rituals

Holy Oils Each year during Holy Week, there is a solemn ritual at the cathedral church. During the ritual, the holy oils used in the parishes throughout the coming year are consecrated by the bishop at the Chrism Mass. These oils are the Sacred Chrism, a mixture of olive oil and fragrant balm, used in Baptism, Confirmation, and Holy Orders; the Oil of Catechumens used to anoint adults preparing for Baptism; and the Oil of the Sick, used in the Sacrament of the Anointing of the Sick. Parish representatives return to their churches with the consecrated oils, to be used in the celebration of Sacraments throughout the year.

St. Augustine's Cathedral in Tuscon, Arizona

14 We Celebrate the Gift of the Holy Spirit

 O God, send your Holy Spirit to help and guide us.

Based on the Rite of Confirmation

Share

Water and oil are used in many ways. Circle the sign for water or oil under each picture.

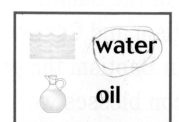
water
oil

How does the Church use water and oil?

Hear & Believe

Worship The Gift of the Holy Spirit

We receive the gift of the Holy Spirit in the Sacraments. Two of the Sacraments are Baptism and Confirmation.

In Baptism the priest or deacon blesses water before he pours it on the person. He prays, "Father, by the power of the Holy Spirit, we ask you now to bless this water. May it wash away all sin and give us new life in Christ."

Based on the Rite of Baptism for Children

In Confirmation the bishop uses holy oil to make the sign of the cross on the forehead of the person. He says, "Be sealed with the Gift of the Holy Spirit." This means, "Be filled with God's Spirit."

Based on the Rite of Confirmation

164

The Holy Spirit Comes to Us

The Holy Spirit comes to us in the **Sacraments**. The Church celebrates Sacraments as signs of God's love. In each Sacrament, the Holy Spirit gives us grace. This gift of grace helps us follow Jesus.

Our Church Teaches

In Baptism, we are washed clean of all sin. The Holy Spirit fills us with God's love. The Holy Spirit helps us live as good Catholics.

In **Confirmation** the Holy Spirit makes our faith stronger. The holy oil is a sign that the Holy Spirit is working in us.

How else can the Holy Spirit help us?

Respond

The Story of Nicodemus

One night, Nicodemus went secretly to Jesus. "What must I do to become a member of God's family?" he asked Jesus.

Jesus said, "You must be born of water and the Spirit."

"How can this happen?" Nicodemus asked.

Jesus explained, "If you believe in me, the Holy Spirit will bring you God's own life. This life will last forever."

"What is this life like?" Nicodemus asked.

Jesus explained, "Instead of living in darkness, you will live in the light. Instead of doing bad things, you will do what is good."

Based on John 3:1–21

? What do you think Nicodemus did next?

Activity

The Holy Spirit
guides us to make
good choices.
Look at each picture.
Read the sentences.
Draw a line under
the better choice.

Please take out the garbage.

Lisa watches TV.
Lisa takes out the garbage.

It's my turn to play.

Tim keeps playing with the truck.
Tim lets Bruce play with the truck.

Pray with us.

Rosa tries to sing and pray.
Rosa plays with her toys.

How can we
pray to the
Holy Spirit?

✝ Prayer Celebration

A Prayer to the Holy Spirit

Special prayers are said when holy oil is used in the Sacraments. We can pray with oil, too. The oil reminds us that the Holy Spirit is with us.

Leader: Let us call upon the Holy Spirit to help us follow Jesus.

All: Holy Spirit, help us and guide us.

Leader: (rubs oil on each child's hands) The Holy Spirit lives in you. What is your prayer?

Child: Holy Spirit, help me and guide me.

A **Circle** the word that best completes each sentence.

1. We are washed clean of all sin in ____.
   Confirmation   (Baptism)

2. Special signs of God's love are called ____.
   prayers   (Sacraments)

3. The Sacrament that makes our faith stronger is ____.
   (Confirmation)   Penance and Reconciliation

4. Jesus told Nicodemus that God's life lasts ____.
   (forever)   ten years

B **Draw or write** about a time when the Holy Spirit helped you.

He helps me when I'm sick

Faith in Action

Servers at Mass Altar servers help priests and deacons celebrate Mass. Boys and girls can usually become altar servers in the fourth grade. An altar server carries the crucifix to lead the procession. Servers light the candles. They also help set the altar for Mass.

In Your Parish

Activity In each corner of the maze there is something to bring to the altar. Draw a line along the right path from each object to the altar.

In Everyday Life

Activity Name two ways that you can help, or serve, your family at home. Name two ways you can help, or serve, at school.

Take Home

FAMILY TIME

The Holy Spirit Is Our Helper

In this chapter the children will come to understand that the Holy Spirit helps us follow Jesus. They will learn the Fruits of the Holy Spirit from Paul's letter to one of the early Christian communities. As the children use their good habits to show love for others, they will begin to realize that the Holy Spirit is acting in their lives.

ACTIVITY

Seeds of Virtue The family has been called the seedbed of virtue because it is in the family that children learn the good habits necessary for a Christian life. Purchase an envelope of seeds and make labels with the names of good habits you would like for your child. Together plant the seeds and watch them grow.

Patience   Generosity   Kindness

WEEKLY PLANNER

On Sunday

During the Prayer of the Faithful, ask the Holy Spirit to help you develop habits that will make you more loving.

On the Web

www.blestarewe.com

 Visit our Web site for the Saint of the day and the reflection question of the week.

Saint of the Week

 Saint Paul
(first century)

Paul, a Jew originally named Saul, vowed that he would arrest Jesus' followers, the Christians. After hearing Jesus' voice, Saul experienced his own conversion. Paul spent the rest of his life telling others about Jesus. In his letters, Paul tells how the Holy Spirit helps us follow Jesus.

Feast Day: January 25.

A Prayer for the Week

Loving God, you send us your Spirit to help us follow Jesus. You help us to be loving, gentle, and kind. We promise to use our good habits to help others. Amen.

Take Home

FAMILY TIME

✝ Scripture Background

In the Time of the Early Church

Letter to the Galatians Paul wrote letters, or Epistles, to some of the early Christian communities as well as to individual disciples. His letter to the Galatians, which includes the Fruits of the Holy Spirit, emphasizes the absolute importance of Christ and his Cross as the way to Salvation and holiness. It stresses Christian freedom and the perfecting of Mosaic Law. Whereas, Mosaic Law provided the Israelites with meticulous observance of ritual, social, and moral regulations; the new law presented a vision of the life of grace in Christ with the help of the Holy Spirit. You may wish to read all six chapters of Paul's letter.

OUR CATHOLIC TRADITION in Theology

St. Thomas Aquinas Thomas Aquinas, who lived in the thirteenth century, became known as one of the best thinkers in history. He greatly influenced theological thought in the Western Church. Aquinas developed a theology of the Holy Spirit based on his understanding of the gifts in Isaiah 11:2–3 and the fruits in Galatians 5:22–23. He taught not only that we should use the Spirit's power and gifts in our lives, but that we should truly enjoy and feel close to the Holy Spirit, just as we do with a dear friend.

Aquinas believed that the Spirit's peace and joy make us content and that these fruits transform our hearts, changing fear and anxiety into security and the desire to give to others.

15 The Holy Spirit Is Our Helper

 **LET US PRAY** Let us follow the Holy Spirit.

Based on Galatians 5:25

Share

Some things we do are habits. Our habits can be good or bad. To brush our teeth every day is a good habit. To bite our nails is a bad habit.

Write a **G** in the box before Nick and Jenny's good habits. Write a **B** in the box before Nick and Jenny's bad habits.

☐ Jenny puts her toys away before bedtime.

☐ Nick always leaves his jacket on the floor.

☐ Nick says "thank you" when he gets a gift.

☐ Jenny prays to God each day.

☐ Jenny slams the door every morning.

How does the Holy Spirit help us learn good habits?

Hear & Believe

✝ Scripture A Letter from Paul

Paul became a follower of Jesus Christ. He wrote this letter to a group of the first **Christians** .

My Dear People,
Jesus Christ loves you. He wants you to love others the way you love yourselves. Sometimes it will be hard to be kind and helpful. But Christ gave you the Holy Spirit to be your helper and guide.
If you follow the Spirit, the Fruits of the Holy Spirit will be yours. You will act with love, joy, and peace. You will be patient, gentle, and kind. You will have self-control.

Based on Galatians 5:14–25

Kindness   JOY   Love

The Holy Spirit Helps Us

Paul's letter is about loving others. Jesus knew that it would not always be easy to love. That is why Jesus gave us the Holy Spirit. When we love others, the Holy Spirit helps us to be joyful, peaceful, patient, gentle, and kind. He helps us to use self-control.

Our Church Teaches

When we practice good habits, we share the **Fruits of the Holy Spirit** with others. These fruits are signs that the Holy Spirit is acting in our lives. When we do kind acts again and again, kindness becomes a habit. Our kindness teaches others about the kindness of God.

We Believe

The Holy Spirit helps us follow Jesus. The Holy Spirit helps us learn good habits of showing love for others.

Faith Words

Christians
Christians are people who love Jesus Christ and follow him.

Fruits of the Holy Spirit
The Fruits of the Holy Spirit are signs that he is acting in our lives.

How can we use the Fruits of the Holy Spirit?

Peace Patience Gentleness

Respond

Tony's Saturday Habit

Tony is fun to play with. He shares his toys. He helps younger children learn new games. He stops fights by saying funny things. Everyone feels good when Tony is around.
But, Tony has a Saturday habit. He watches TV for three hours. All his friends want him to come out and play. But Tony says, "I can't. I need to watch my shows."

 What do you think about Tony's habit?

love

joy

176

Activities

1. Pick a Fruit of the Holy Spirit and circle it. Draw how you will use this fruit with someone at home.

peace

patience

self-control

gentleness

kindness

2. Pick another Fruit of the Holy Spirit and draw a box around it. Write about how you will use this fruit in school.

How can we celebrate the Fruits of the Holy Spirit?

Prayer Celebration

A Prayer for Help

We pray to the Holy Spirit to help us learn good habits. We pray that the Holy Spirit will help us show love for others.

Leader: Let us pray to the Holy Spirit, our helper and guide.

Side 1: When a new child moves into our neighborhood,

Side 2: Help us show kindness.

Side 1: When our friends are sad,

Side 2: Help us bring them joy.

Side 1: When children are fighting,

Side 2: Help us be peacemakers.

Side 1: When someone is hurting,

Side 2: Help us be gentle.

All: Holy Spirit, fill us with your love. Help us follow Jesus.

Complete the sentences with words from the box.

Fruits joy Christians kind Jesus Christ

1. People who love and follow Jesus Christ

_____

- -

are called _____.

2. Paul's letter tells us that

_____

- -

_____ loves us.

3. The _____ of the
Holy Spirit are signs that he is acting
in our lives.

4. The Holy Spirit helps us to be

_____

- -

_____ to others.

5. The Holy Spirit helps us share our love

_____

- -

and _____ with others.

Faith in Action

Youth Group Many parishes have a group for teens. The teens make new friends, serve their community, and learn more about God. Some teens visit the sick. Some collect clothes for the poor. Others rake leaves or shovel snow for older members of the parish.

In Your Parish

Activity Does your parish have a youth group? How do the teens help people?

In Everyday Life

Activity
The Holy Spirit helps us act in good ways. Read the signs. Circle one way that you would like to act. Then draw yourself acting in this way.

Help a friend.

Pray every day.

Obey your parents.

Forgive others.

Share your toys.

Take Home

FAMILY TIME

The Holy Spirit Helps Us Pray

In this chapter the children will read some of Jesus' teachings about prayer that are in the Bible. They will learn that the Holy Spirit teaches us how to pray for the things we need. Each child will write a prayer of petition to the Holy Spirit, and will participate in a Holy Spirit prayer celebration.

ACTIVITY

A Prayer Box Decorate a small, empty box with symbols of the Holy Spirit, such as doves and flames of fire. Leave blank pieces of paper next to the box. Invite your family to write petitions on the papers and to place them in the prayer box. Together, read the petitions and pray for each other's requests.

WEEKLY PLANNER

On Sunday

During Mass, listen to the readings and prayers for times when the Holy Spirit is mentioned. On your way home, discuss some of these times.

On the Web

www.blestarewe.com

 Visit our Web site for the Saint of the day and the reflection question of the week.

Saint of the Week

 **Saint Clare**
(1193–1253)

Clare, a friend and follower of Francis of Assisi, came from a wealthy Italian family. She joined Francis in living a life of poverty and simplicity. Francis helped Clare found a religious community of women known as the Poor Clares. The sisters live a very disciplined lifestyle in their efforts to help the poor.

Feast Day: August 11.

A Prayer for the Week

Come Holy Spirit, fill our family with your love. Help us place our trust in Jesus and show our love for others as Saint Clare did. Amen.

Take Home

FAMILY TIME

✝ Scripture Background

In the Time of Jesus

Petitions Prayers of petition are requests made to God. Jesus speaks of praying for one's needs and for the healing of the sick. He speaks of praying for ourselves and for others. Within the prayer of petition, however, is the understanding that while these prayers are offered to God in faith and expectation, through Christ and the Holy Spirit, God's responses are based on his will and what is best for the kingdom. Some of Jesus' teachings about prayer of petition can be found in Matthew 6:5–15; 7:7–11.

OUR CATHOLIC TRADITION in Liturgy

The Holy Spirit's Role in Liturgy Prayers to the Holy Spirit reveal the Spirit's role in the liturgical life of the Church. During the Eucharistic Prayer at Mass, we petition God to send the Holy Spirit as Sanctifier to change the bread and wine and to change us, so that we too, become holy and united in the Body of Christ.

The principal prayers of the Sacraments reveal more about the Holy Spirit's role. In Baptism, we pray to the Holy Spirit for new life. In Confirmation, we ask the Spirit to be our helper and guide.

In Reconciliation, we ask the Holy Spirit, as Comforter, to forgive our sins. Through the Holy Spirit, we are given the grace to lead a Christian life.

16 The Holy Spirit Helps Us Pray

Come, Holy Spirit,
fill our hearts with your love.

Based on the Pentecost Sequence

Share

We all need teachers.
Teachers help us learn
new words.
Teachers show us how to
do new things.

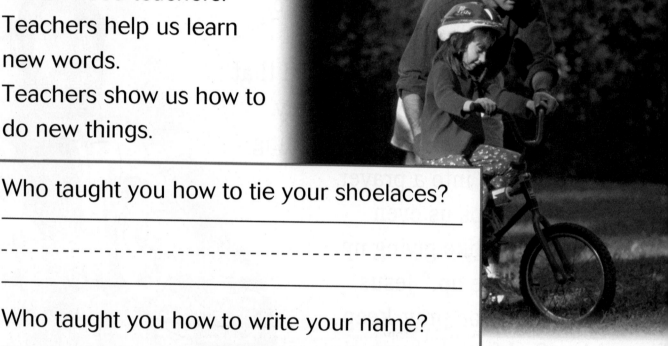

Who taught you how to tie your shoelaces?

_____

- -

_____

Who taught you how to write your name?

_____

- -

_____

Who taught you how to ride a bike?

_____

- -

_____

Who taught you about Jesus?

_____

- -

_____

How does the
Holy Spirit
help us pray?

Hear & Believe

✝ Scripture A Special Teacher

Jesus told his friends many stories about prayer. One time Jesus said that we should pray always.

"How can we do that?" people asked. "We will grow tired. We will run out of things to say."

Another time Jesus explained that the Holy Spirit teaches us to pray. This Spirit helps us turn everything we say and do into a prayer. The Spirit helps us even when we feel like giving up.

"Never give up," Jesus said. "When you pray, keep asking God for what you need. Keep knocking at God's door until he answers. For everyone who asks, receives. Everyone who seeks, finds. And to everyone who knocks, the door is opened."

Based on Luke 18:1, Romans 8:26, Ephesians 6:18, and Matthew 7:7–8

Ways the Holy Spirit Helps Us

The Holy Spirit teaches us to pray. He helps us pray for what we need. We call these prayers **petitions**. Even our kind acts can become prayers. Helping a person shows our love for God. Our kind act becomes a prayer.

Our Church Teaches

At Mass, we pray to the Holy Spirit many times. He helps us listen to the Bible stories. The Holy Spirit changes the bread and wine into the Body and Blood of Christ. He helps us become holy. After Mass the Holy Spirit helps us love others.

We Believe

The Holy Spirit helps us pray in many ways. Even the good things we do can become prayers.

Faith Words

petitions
Petitions are asking prayers. We ask God to give us the things we need.

How does the Church honor the Holy Spirit?

Respond

The Holy Parade

Lucia and her grandfather are on the church steps. She hears joyful music from a band. Then she sees the marchers coming down the street

The men and boys wear colorful shirts and vests. The women and girls wear long dresses. Each group carries a bright banner.

Lucia asks, "Why are they marching?"

"It is a holy parade, or procession," her grandfather replies. "Every year, we honor the Holy Spirit in a special way. At Mass today, we will thank God for the gift of the Holy Spirit."

? Why are the people having a procession?

Activity

Write a petition to the Holy Spirit.
Ask the Holy Spirit to help you.
Then sign your name.

LOVE

gentleness

Come, Holy Spirit,

_____

- -

fill me with _____.

_____

- -

Help me to _____

_____

- -

_____.

My name is

_____

- -

_____.

peace

self-control

JOY

kindness

patience

How can we celebrate the Holy Spirit?

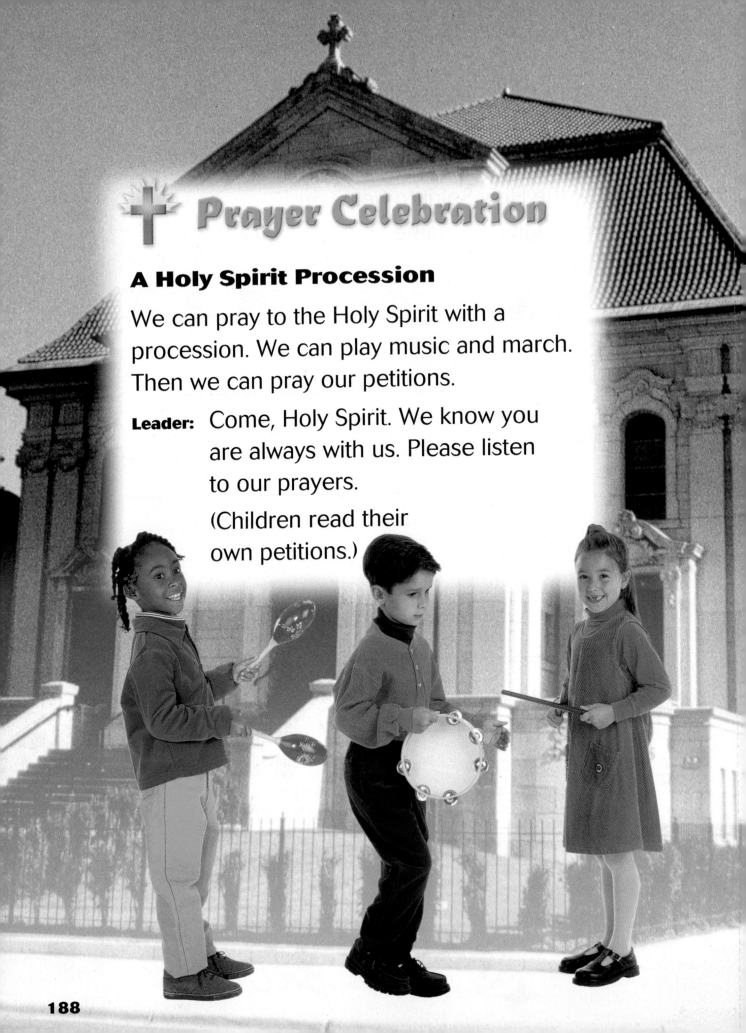

✝ Prayer Celebration

A Holy Spirit Procession

We can pray to the Holy Spirit with a procession. We can play music and march. Then we can pray our petitions.

Leader: Come, Holy Spirit. We know you are always with us. Please listen to our prayers.

(Children read their own petitions.)

A **Circle** the word that best completes each sentence.

1. Helping others can be a way to ____.
   laugh   **pray**

2. Prayers that ask God for things we need are called ____.
   petitions   **praises**

3. Jesus said that we should pray ____.
   sometimes   **always**

4. The Holy Spirit teaches us to ____.
   pray   **play**

B **Write** a petition to the Holy Spirit.

Come Holy Spirit,

_____

_____

_____

_____

Faith in Action

Prayer Box Many parishes have a "Prayer Box." People write petitions on small cards and put them in the box. When a prayer group meets, the members read some of the petitions. Then the group prays for the needs of the people.

In Your Parish

Activity How does your parish pray for the needs of its people? Is there a prayer box? Find out. Then you can pray for people's needs, too.

In Everyday Life

Activity Look at the Prayer Chain. On each link, write the name of a person who needs prayers. Then pray for these people.

Prayer Chain

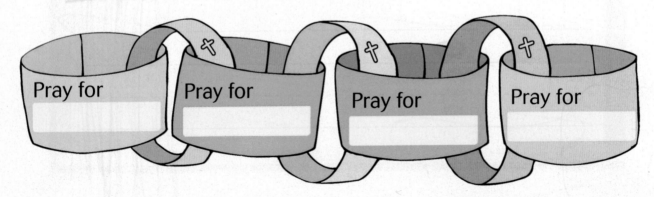

Pray for

Pray for

Pray for

Pray for

Jesus' Church of Followers

The Catholic Church throughout the world helps people in need. These people are our brothers and sisters. As baptized Christians, we are called to love and serve others.

Go into the whole world. Share the good news about Jesus with everyone.

Based on Mark 16:15

CLOTHING DRIVE

Early Christians traveled this road to faraway countries. They helped people learn about Jesus. These children are helping by sending clothes to needy people around the world.

Laudate Dominum

Psalm 117, "Praise the Lord, all you peoples."

Music by Jacques Berthier

OSTINATO REFRAIN

Lau - da - te Do - mi-num, lau - da - te Do - mi-num

om - nes gen-tes, al - le - lu - ia. al - le - lu - ia.

Take Home

FAMILY TIME

Jesus' Followers Become the Church

In this chapter the children will learn that Jesus invites his followers to belong to the Church. From the Scripture story, the children will discover that the first Christians prayed together, celebrated the Eucharist, and helped poor people. The children will also learn that the word, *Amen*, means, "Yes, I believe. It is true."

ACTIVITY

Family Traditions Tell your children stories about relatives who were role models for the way your family prays, celebrates, and helps others. If you have letters or photos about these traditions, share them with your children.

WEEKLY PLANNER

On Sunday

Discuss how your church building is like a home for your parish community.

On the Web

www.blestarewe.com

 Visit our Web site for the Saint of the day and the reflection question of the week.

Saint of the Week

 Saint Peter the Apostle (first century)

Peter, a fisherman, was called by Jesus to be one of his Twelve Apostles. Jesus loved Peter very much, in spite of Peter's denial about knowing him during the Passion. After the Resurrection, Jesus made Peter leader of the Apostles and head of the Church. Peter was later arrested in Rome and put to death.

Feast Day: February 22

 **A Prayer for the Week**

Lord Jesus Christ, we thank you for calling us to be your followers. Send us your Spirit to fill us with joy and to help us share our love with others. Amen.

Take Home

✝ Scripture Background

In the Time of the Early Church

Eucharist   Scripture provides few details about how the Eucharist, or Lord's Supper, was celebrated in the first Christian communities (Acts 2:42–47; 20:7; 27:35; 1 Corinthians 10:16; 11:17–34). From these brief accounts, we sense that the disciples were filled with the joy of the Resurrection and the hope of the Second Coming. Gathering in someone's home for a communal meal, they blessed and thanked God and recalled the events of Jesus' life, Death, and Resurrection. By repeating Jesus' words of consecration at the Last Supper, he became present to them in the breaking of the bread.

OUR CATHOLIC TRADITION in Architecture

Domed Churches   In Eastern Christianity the churches are usually topped with domes instead of steeples. These domes are often gilded, expressing the radiance of Heaven. One of the most famous of the domed churches is the Cathedral of St. Basil in Moscow, Russia. Building began in the sixteenth century during the reign of Czar Ivan IV. Many colorful, onion shaped domes are covered with intricate patterns. Gold is used heavily in the decoration.

17 Jesus' Followers Become the Church

 Jesus' followers were filled with joy and the Holy Spirit.

Based on Acts 13:52

Share

Our friends bring joy to our lives.

We can do things with our friends.

We can share things with our friends.

We can tell our friends how we feel.

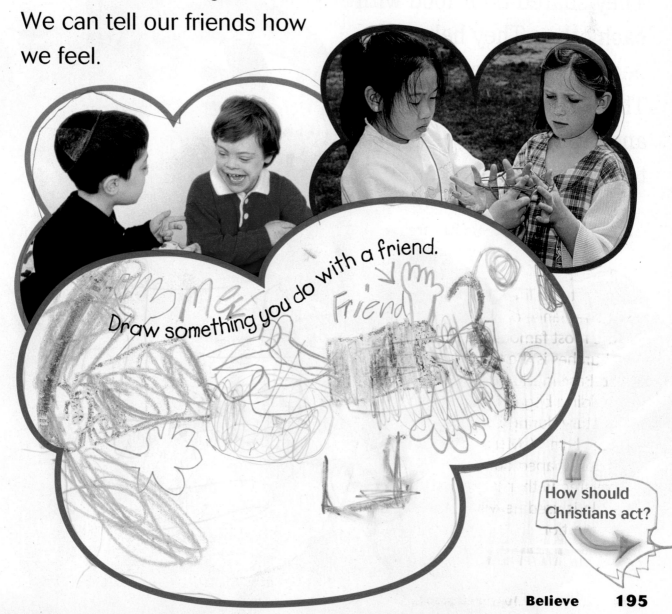

Draw something you do with a friend.

How should Christians act?

Hear & Believe

✝ Scripture The First Christians

After Christ rose from the dead, many people began to believe in him. They became his followers. Here is what these first Christians did.

They listened to the Apostles. They tried to live and act like Jesus. They prayed together and celebrated the Eucharist. They shared their food with each other. They helped people who were poor. They grew in faith and brought joy to one another.

Based on Acts 2:42–47

Acting as Christians

The followers of Jesus became the first members of the Church. They loved one another. Their **faith**, or belief in God, was strong. Jesus calls us, too, to be members of his Church. When we show love to others, we are true Christians.

Our Church Teaches

Amen is a prayer often prayed by the first Christians. We pray "Amen" many times at Mass. We pray "Amen" at the end of prayers we say each day. "Amen" means "Yes, I believe. It is true."

Faith Words
faith
Faith is belief and trust in God.

Amen
Amen means "Yes, I believe. It is true." We often say "Amen" at the end of prayers.

How can we act like the first Christians?

Respond

Saint Paul's Parish

The people of Saint Paul's parish try to act like the first Christians. Here are some ways they show love to others.

Mrs. Santos teaches children about Jesus.

Nancy prays with others.

Vanessa takes care of young children.

Activity

There are six words in the church-window Word Search.

The words tell how Christians try to act.

Find the words and circle them.

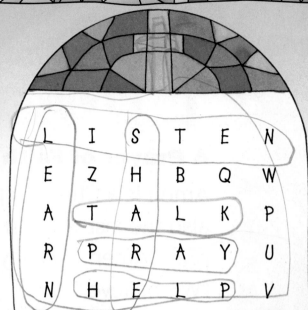

L I S T E N
E Z H B Q W
A T A L K P
R P R A Y U
N H E L P V

Ryan listens to a friend

Mrs. Carr helps people who are poor.

Mr. Smith drives senior citizens to lunch.

How can we pray "Amen"?

✝ Prayer Celebration

A Prayer of Faith

Amen is a Christian prayer of faith. It is also the last word in some Bibles. When we pray "Amen," we say "yes" to God. We say, "We believe."

Let us pray "Amen" to what we believe.

Reader 1: Thank you, God, for the gift of the Church. We believe you want us to belong to the Catholic Church.

All: Amen.

Reader 2: Thank you, God, for the gift of creation. We believe you know us and care for us.

All: Amen.

Reader 3: Thank you, God, for the gift of Jesus. We believe he is your Son.

All: Amen.

Reader 4: Thank you, God, for the gift of the Holy Spirit. We believe your Spirit is always with us.

All: Amen.

A **Draw** lines to the words that best complete the sentences.

1. The first Christians tried to live and act ●   ● the Church.

2. Belief and trust in God is called ●   ● like Jesus.

3. We end prayers with the word, ●   ● faith.

4. Jesus' followers became members of ●   ● Amen.

B **Write or draw** how you can act as a Christian.

Faith in Action

Job-Finding Helpers   If someone needs a job, Mount Carmel Parish tries to help. The parish Web site lists many job openings. A person can sign up on the Web site. The job-finding group can help a person learn new skills. That can help the person get a job.

In Your Parish

Activity   Mr. Mann lost his job as a carpenter. His wife is ill and cannot work. Their children need clothes. How could your parish help?

In Everyday Life

Activity   The words in the box name our rights. Find and circle each right in the Word Search.

food

shoes

home

school

doctor

job

c o f o o d i u
z s o b r o g y
y c i f q c s p
k h o m e t j z
k o e h j o b d
y o o j n r l o
j l z o e c s u
l o s h o e s z

Take Home

FAMILY TIME

We Celebrate Pentecost

In this chapter, children will recognize the Feast of Pentecost as the birthday of the Church. They will hear the Scripture story of how the Holy Spirit filled Jesus' followers with the gift of God's love. The children will discover that people from all over the world belong to the Catholic Church, and will discuss what it means to live in peace.

ACTIVITY

A Pentecost Mobile With your child, make a Pentecost mobile out of a hanger, thread, and red and white construction paper. Cut out a white dove and red flames. Label each flame with a family member's name. Using thread, hang the dove and flames from the hanger. The dove symbolizes God's power to make us holy, and the flames represent the outpouring of the Holy Spirit.

WEEKLY PLANNER

On Sunday

Find out how your parish plans to celebrate Pentecost by asking a member of the parish staff or looking in the parish bulletin.

On the Web

www.blestarewe.com

 Visit our Web site for the Saint of the day and the reflection question of the week.

Saint of the Week

Saint Francis Xavier (1506–1552)

Francis Xavier grew up in Spain and studied in Paris. He helped his friend, Ignatius found the Society of Jesus, or Jesuits. Francis worked with the poor and sick in India and Japan. He learned their languages and baptized over one thousand people.

Patron Saint of: missionaries in foreign lands
Feast Day: December 3

A Prayer for the Week

God our Father, we thank you for sending us your Holy Spirit. Help our family follow the example of Saint Francis Xavier by telling others about the Good News of Jesus. Amen.

Take Home

FAMILY TIME

✝ Scripture Background

In the Time of the Early Church

Pentecost   In the Old Testament, Pentecost was celebrated as the Feast of Weeks. It began as an agricultural feast, showing gratitude to God for the early harvest. The feast was held fifty days after the first day of Passover. In the New Testament, Christians began to celebrate Pentecost as a commemoration of the day the Church was born. On this day the Holy Spirit came to the Apostles and empowered them to speak in tongues. People from many countries were able to understand the Good News about Jesus in their own languages.

You can read the account of the first Pentecost in Acts 2:1–42.

OUR CATHOLIC TRADITION   in Culture

Pentecost Around the World
The celebration of Pentecost differs around the world. In Italy it was customary to throw down rose leaves from church ceilings to symbolize the fiery tongues. In France, trumpets were blown to recall the sound of the mighty wind that came with the descent of the Holy Spirit.

Today in Eastern Catholic Churches, the Vespers of Pentecost includes a ritual of genuflection. In Russia, people carry flowers and green branches in a procession. The photo shows pilgrims journeying to the annual Pentecost festival held in El Rocio in southern Spain.

18 We Celebrate Pentecost

LET US PRAY

The Spirit of the Lord fills the whole world.

Based on Wisdom 1:7

Share

Birthdays are very special days.
Our families and friends celebrate with us.
They are glad that we belong to them.
When is your birthday?

_____

- -

_____

Month   **Day**

Circle the things that were part of your last birthday celebration.

Draw another special thing that was at your birthday celebration.

When does the Church celebrate its birthday?

Hear & Believe

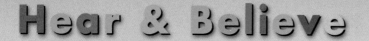

Worship The Church's Birthday

A reading from the Acts of the Apostles

Fifty days after Easter, Jesus' followers were praying together. Suddenly there was a sound like a great wind blowing. The noise filled the whole house. Then flames, like tongues of fire, appeared over each person's head. The Holy Spirit filled all the people in the house with God's love. The Apostles and the others rushed outside. They began telling everyone about Jesus.

Outside there were people from many countries. These people spoke different languages. But they all understood what Jesus' followers were saying. That day the Church was born!

Based on Acts 2:1–6

Reader: The word of the Lord.

All: Thanks be to God.

Pentecost Sunday

We celebrate the birthday of the Church on **Pentecost** Sunday. We remember how Jesus' followers were filled with the Holy Spirit. We remember that the Holy Spirit helped them teach people from many countries about Jesus.

Our Church Teaches

The Church welcomes people of all races, languages, and abilities. Today people all over the world belong to the Church. As Catholics, we try to live in **peace** with everyone.

How can we live in peace with everyone?

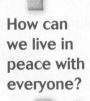

Respond

The Special Sunday

Pentecost is a special Sunday in Sylvia's parish. The children are invited to walk in a procession. They carry flags from many countries. Sylvia carries a flag from Mexico. Her friend, Ravi, carries an Indian flag. The flags remind everyone that the Church is made up of people from all over the world.

During Mass, the people sing in different languages. After Mass, everyone goes outside to eat foods and play games from different countries.

? What did the people in Sylvia's parish celebrate on Pentecost?

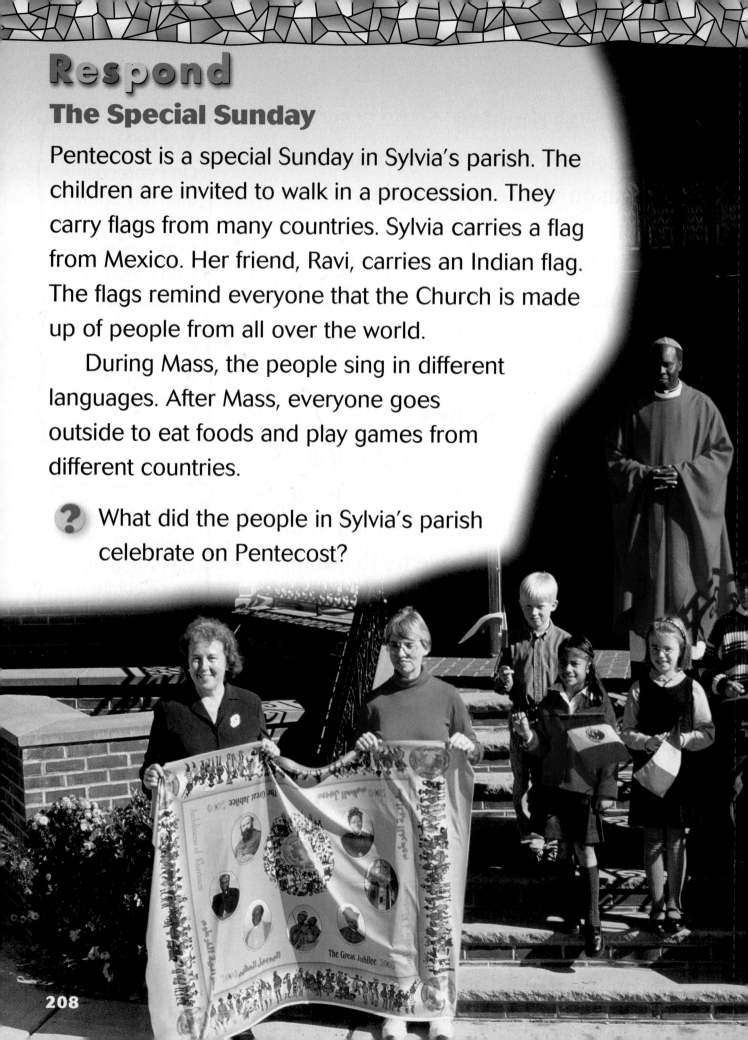

Activity

1. Many different people make up the Church.
   Many colors make
   a beautiful picture.
   Use this code to
   color the picture.
   What do you see?

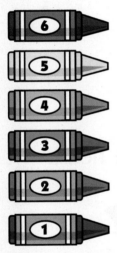

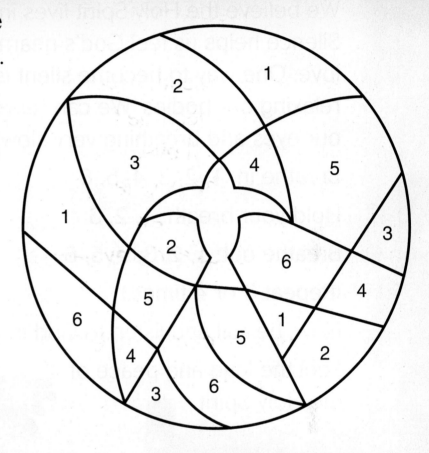

2. Circle the words that tell ways to keep peace.

   You are playing a game with a friend.

   cheat   play fair

   A friend calls you names.

   forgive   act mad

   There is one toy, but three people.

   take it   share it

   A family member needs you.

   help   watch TV

How can we
celebrate
the Church's
birthday?

✝ Prayer Celebration

A Silent Prayer

We believe the Holy Spirit lives in us. Silence helps us feel God's nearness and love. One way to become silent is by relaxing our bodies. We can relax by closing our eyes and breathing very slowly.

Breathe in. 1, 2, 3, 4, 5, 6

Hold your breath: 1, 2, 3

Breathe out: 1, 2, 3, 4, 5, 6

(Repeat 3 or 4 times.)

Now, be still and listen to God in your heart.

Feel the love and peace of the Holy Spirit.

Complete the sentences with words from the box.

Holy Spirit   Jesus   Pentecost   peace   Apostles

1. The birthday of the Church is called

_____

- -

_____.

2. Pentecost celebrates the coming of the

_____

- -

_____.

3. The Holy Spirit filled the followers of

_____

- -

_____ with God's love.

4. The Holy Spirit helped the

_____

- -

_____ teach

people of all countries about Jesus.

5. Silent prayer can help us feel the love and

_____

- -

_____ of the Holy Spirit.

Faith in Action

Readers of God's Word At Mass, we listen to readings from the Bible. The people who read the Word of God are called lectors. At home, they learn about the Bible stories. They practice reading the stories aloud. The lectors want us to hear God's message. They want us to believe the words we hear.

In Your Parish

Activity On Pentecost a lector reads aloud the Bible story about the coming of the Holy Spirit.
Circle the words in the box that are in the Pentecost story. Then tell the story in your own words.

fifty days   Christmas   followers   water
flames   Easter
eating   praying   wind   God's love
children   animals
Apostles   Holy Spirit   people
Jesus
languages   Church
Temple   born

In Everyday Life

Activity Choose a favorite Bible story from your book. Read the story to yourself. Then pretend you are a lector. Read the Word of God to others.

Take Home

FAMILY TIME

The Church Helps the World

Our Church teaches that all the people in the world are our brothers and sisters. In this chapter the children will learn that our mission as Christians is to love and serve others. They will discover how Catholics have answered God's call to help people all over the world. The children will become aware of ways they can help people in need, and of the importance of praying for our Church's "helpers."

ACTIVITY

Cards Full of Cheer Help your child make cheerful cards for children in a hospital or elderly people in a nursing home. Deliver the cards yourselves, or give the cards to someone in your parish who will deliver them.

WEEKLY PLANNER

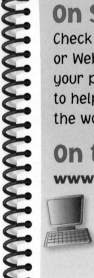

On Sunday

Check your parish's bulletin or Web site to find out how your parish is reaching out to help poor people around the world.

On the Web

www.blestarewe.com

Visit our Web site for the Saint of the day and the reflection question of the week.

Saint of the Week

Blessed Teresa of Calcutta (1910–1997)

Born in Yugoslavia, Mother Teresa entered the Sisters of Loreto and became a high school teacher in Calcutta, India. In 1948 she felt God calling her to serve the poorest of the poor, and founded the Missionaries of Charity. Today its members serve the poor, sick, and dying around the world.

Feast Day: September 5

A Prayer for the Week

Lord, we want to help people in need. Help us to be your hands and feet in the world today. Give us courage to answer your call to serve others. Amen.

Take Home

FAMILY TIME

✝ Scripture Background

In the Time of the Early Church

The Role of Deacons   As the early Church grew in numbers, the Apostles found they were no longer able to see to all the needs of the faithful. Therefore, they asked the disciples to choose several reputable men from the community to assist them. The Apostles ordained those chosen as deacons. The deacons performed services connected to the ritual of the Lord's Supper, such as serving and cleaning up. They also cared for the needs of widows and orphans.

You can read more about deacons in 1 Timothy 3:8–13.

Our Catholic Tradition   in Holy People

A Witness to the Poor
Dorothy Day was a convert to Catholicism who had a strong sense of the social call of the Gospel. She reached out to the poor and powerless and gave of herself with great dignity. She started Catholic Worker houses across the country, and encouraged people to follow Christ.

One group of people Dorothy ministered to was women prisoners. While she was visiting a West Virginia prison, an elderly inmate wanted to know why Dorothy was there. She replied that she had come to wash their feet. Dorothy Day died in 1980. She was a powerful witness to the Church's mission of serving the poor.

19 The Church Helps the World

LET US PRAY Go into the whole world. Share the good news about Jesus with everyone.

Based on Mark 16:15

Share

Before we can help others, we must find out what they need. Look at these pictures. What do the people need?

He needs

_____

- -

_____.

They need

_____

- -

_____.

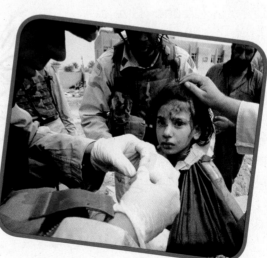

She needs

_____

- - - - - - - - - - - - - - - - -

_____.

Why should Christians help people in need?

Hear & Believe

✝ Scripture The Need for Helpers

The Church of Jesus' followers grew quickly. There was too much work for the Apostles to do by themselves. So they asked the community to choose helpers. Some of these helpers were Stephen, Philip, and Nicholas. Stephen was good at telling people about God's Word in the Bible. The others made sure the people had food, clothes, and a place to live.

Then the Apostles had time to tell more people about Jesus. They had more time to lead people in prayer and to start new communities.

Based on Acts 6:1–7

Christian Service

The first Christians learned that God calls everyone to help and **serve** others. They took care of everyone in their community. Helping people is our **mission**, too. When we take care of the needs of others, we follow Jesus.

Our Church Teaches

All the people in the world are our brothers and sisters. Many people need help. Each baptized person is called to love and serve others. The Holy Spirit helps us serve others with love, peace, and joy.

We Believe

All people in the world are our brothers and sisters. That is why God asks us to help people in need.

Faith Words

mission
Our mission as Christians is to love and serve others.

How can we live in peace with everyone?

Respond

Catholics Help Others

The Catholic Church helps people all over the world. Some Catholics serve in countries far away. They help people by giving them food, clothes, and medicine. They teach people how to read and write. They tell people about Jesus.

Some Catholics serve in our own country. They build houses for the poor. They serve food to homeless people. They also teach people about Jesus.

? How can we help our Church's helpers?

Activity

1. Draw how you will help someone in need this week.

2. Write a prayer for Church helpers who serve the needs of others.

How can we get ready to be God's helpers?

Prayer Celebration

Saying Yes to God

Leader: As you grow up, God asks you to love and serve others. Are you listening? Are you ready to say yes to God?

Let us pray about saying yes to God.

All: **God, our Creator, you called us by name to belong to your Church. As we grow up, help us to hear your voice. Give us the courage to say "yes" to your call. Amen.**

A **Circle** the words that best complete the sentences.

1. God calls everyone to ____ others.

   serve   **hurt**

2. We believe that ____ in the world are our brothers and sisters.

   some people   **all people**

3. As baptized persons, our ____ is to help others.

   mission   **nation**

4. The Holy Spirit helps us serve others with ____.

   gifts and money   **love and joy**

B **Draw or write** about how a Catholic today can answer God's call to serve others.

Family Rosary Group In some parishes, families gather once a week to pray the Rosary. They pray for peace in the world. Each family takes a turn naming a place in the world that needs peace. The children hold up pictures of that place. Then the group prays that peace will come to the people who live there.

In Your Parish

Activity At Sunday Mass, your parish prays for peace in the world. Think of a place that needs peace. Make up your own prayer for peace.

In Everyday Life

Activity Write or draw about a way you can be a peacemaker in your family, school, or neighborhood.

Take Home

FAMILY TIME

We Pray with Holy Songs

By incorporating music into our prayer, we add a new dimension to the way we relate to God. This chapter encourages the children to think of church music as an integral part of our worship experience. They will discover that holy songs are prayers, and that when we sing with our hearts, as well as our voices, we pray twice.

ACTIVITY

Feel the Music   Play a song that your child likes. Have fun listening to the music and singing the words. Dance to the music with your child, expressing how the song makes you feel.

WEEKLY PLANNER

On Sunday

During Mass, listen carefully to the words of the hymns. After Mass, discuss how they relate to the Scripture readings.

On the Web

www.blestarewe.com

 Visit our Web site for the Saint of the day and the reflection question of the week.

Saint of the Week

 Saint Cecilia (Third century)

According to legend, Cecilia, a Christian, lived in Rome at a time of great persecution. It is said that she sang to God in her heart. Cecilia is often pictured playing a harp or an organ. She was martyred because she refused to offer sacrifice to pagan gods. Pope Urban I dedicated a church in her name.

Patron Saint of: musicians
Feast Day: November 22

A Prayer for the Week

Dear God, we thank you for the gift of music. It comforts us when we feel sad and helps us express our joy. Help us lift our hearts and minds to you in song. Amen.

Take Home

FAMILY TIME

✠ Scripture Background

Before the Time of Jesus

Musical Instruments The most frequently mentioned biblical instrument is the shofar, or ram's horn, which is still used in synagogues today. The kinnor, or David's harp, was actually a lyre, used to accompany the praying of the psalms. Instruments mentioned in the New Testament include the harp, the flute, the lyre, the trumpet, and cymbals. The "resounding gong" referred to by Paul in 1 Corinthians 13:1, were actually vases set up to amplify actors' voices in Greek theaters.

You can read about the importance of religious music to the first Christians in Ephesians 5:18–20.

OUR CATHOLIC TRADITION in Music

Sprituals Most African slaves in our country were not allowed to learn how to read or write. Many slaves were converted to Christianity. One way they kept their faith alive was by singing spirituals. These songs, based on Scripture, sustained the slaves in the same way psalms sustained the Israelites during their captivity. The spirituals also helped the slaves pass on their faith. Spirituals are now considered an art form, and one of the original forms of music on this continent. As African Americans became Catholics, they brought with them their rich heritage in these biblically based hymns.

20 We Pray with Holy Songs

My heart is full of joy.
I sing praises to my God.

Based on Psalm 28:7

Share

People sing for many reasons.

Songs put babies to sleep.

Songs remind us of our country.

Songs take away our fears.
Songs celebrate happy times.

What is your favorite song?

_____

- -

_____

Why do
Christians
sing?

Hear & Believe

✝ Scripture Songs of the First Christians

When the first Christians celebrated the Eucharist, they did several things. They read the Bible. They prayed. They received the Body and Blood of Jesus. And they sang songs.

Why did they sing? Here is what Paul told the first Christians.

Be filled with God's Spirit. Sing psalms and hymns to God the Father. Sing your thanks and praise to God in the name of our Lord Jesus Christ.

Based on Ephesians 5:18–19

Praying with Holy Songs

The first Christians sang because the Holy Spirit filled them with joy. Singing helped them to pray.

We pray when we sing **hymns**, or holy songs. Through song, we give God thanks and praise. We ask God for help. We tell God that we want to help others.

Our Church Teaches

When we sing hymns at Mass, we pray with our voices. These holy songs help lift our hearts to God. The words we sing thank and praise God.

How can we sing our thanks and praise to God?

227

Respond

Amanda Loves to Sing

Amanda loves to sing at church. She sings as her parish community gathers to praise God. After the first Bible reading, she sings a psalm. She sings a hymn when people bring the bread and wine to the altar. She prays to God, our Father, when she sings the Lord's Prayer. Amanda sings at Communion time. She also sings at the end of Mass.

Sometimes during the week, Amanda hums the songs from Mass. The music reminds her to give God thanks and praise. It reminds her to live in peace. It helps her love and serve others.

? **What holy songs do you like to hum?**

Activity

Use these words to complete the sentences.
Then write the words in the puzzle.

| hymn | praise | pray | psalm | thanks |

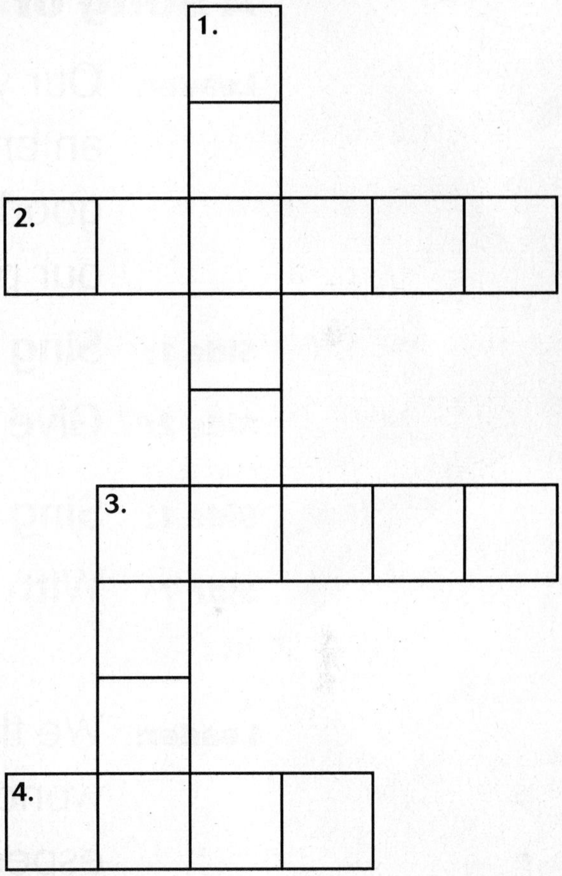

DOWN

1. We give God

t h _ _ _ _ _ _.

3. Singing is a

___ ___ ___ ___ ___

way to ___ ___ ___ ___.

ACROSS

2. By singing, we

___ ___ ___ ___ ___ ___ God.

___ ___ ___ ___ ___ ___

3. A ___ ___ ___ ___ ___ is a song that is
also a prayer.

___ ___ ___ ___

4. A ___ ___ ___ ___ is a holy song.

How can we
celebrate our
good year?

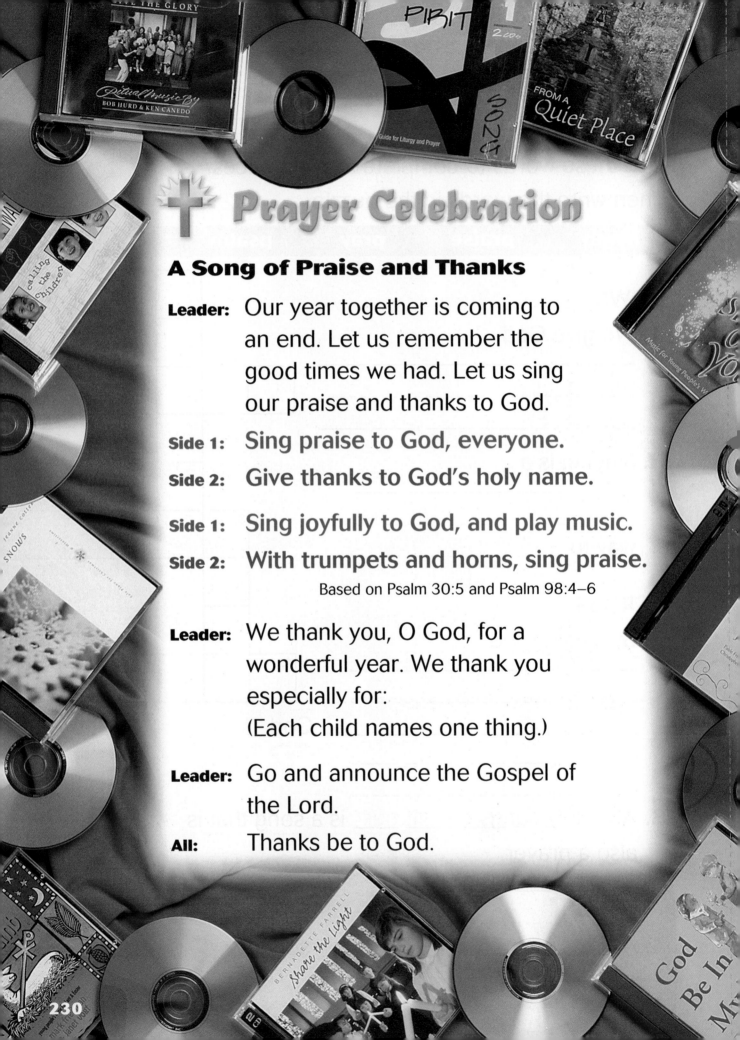

✝ Prayer Celebration

A Song of Praise and Thanks

Leader: Our year together is coming to an end. Let us remember the good times we had. Let us sing our praise and thanks to God.

Side 1: Sing praise to God, everyone.

Side 2: Give thanks to God's holy name.

Side 1: Sing joyfully to God, and play music.

Side 2: With trumpets and horns, sing praise.

Based on Psalm 30:5 and Psalm 98:4–6

Leader: We thank you, O God, for a wonderful year. We thank you especially for:
(Each child names one thing.)

Leader: Go and announce the Gospel of the Lord.

All: Thanks be to God.

A **Draw a line** to the word that best completes each sentence.

1. Holy songs are called   ●   ● praise.

2. When we sing holy songs, we pray   ●   ● hymns.

3. Catholics sing holy songs at   ●   ● twice.

4. Holy songs give God thanks and   ●   ● Mass.

B **Circle** the word that best completes each sentence.

1. Paul told the first Christians to sing _____ to God.
   stories   **psalms**

2. The first Christians sang because the Holy Spirit filled them with _____.
   sorrow   **joy**

3. Holy songs can lift our _____ to God.
   hearts   **hands**

4. Holy songs can remind us to live in _____.
   fear   **peace**

Faith in Action

Music Director   The people in Saint John's Parish love to sing. The music director chooses hymns that go with the Bible readings at Mass. She helps the choir members learn new songs. She tells them to sing from their hearts. She invites everyone to sing praise to God.

In Your Parish

Activity   Write a thank you note to the music director in your parish. Tell how you feel about the holy songs at Mass.

In Everyday Life

Activity   Think about your favorite hymn, or holy song. Very quietly, sing the words to yourself. Tell how this song can help you pray.

FEASTS AND SEASONS

✝ The Church Year

The calendar of the Catholic Church is made up of special seasons. The weeks of each season celebrate the life and teachings of Jesus Christ.

Holy Week begins on Palm Sunday. It ends with three holy days that remind us of the Last Supper, and that Jesus died and rose to new life to save all people.

HOLY WEEK

HOLY WEEK

Our Church year begins on the first Sunday of **Advent**. We have four weeks to get ready to celebrate Jesus' birthday on Christmas.

ADVENT

ADVENT

The Church year begins.

ORDINARY TIME

In the second part of **Ordinary Time**, we learn more about the life and teachings of Jesus.

The **Easter** season is a time of great joy. It begins on Easter Sunday. Easter Time lasts for fifty days. We celebrate that Jesus was raised from the dead. We sing, "Alleluia!"

EASTER

The season of **Lent** begins with Ash Wednesday. During Lent we pray, give up things, and share what we have with others to get ready for Easter.

In the first part of **Ordinary Time**, we learn how Jesus began his work among the people.

LENT   **ORDINARY TIME**

During the **Christmas** season, we celebrate that Jesus, the Son of God, came to Earth as our Savior.

CHRISTMAS

Why Sunday Is a Special Day

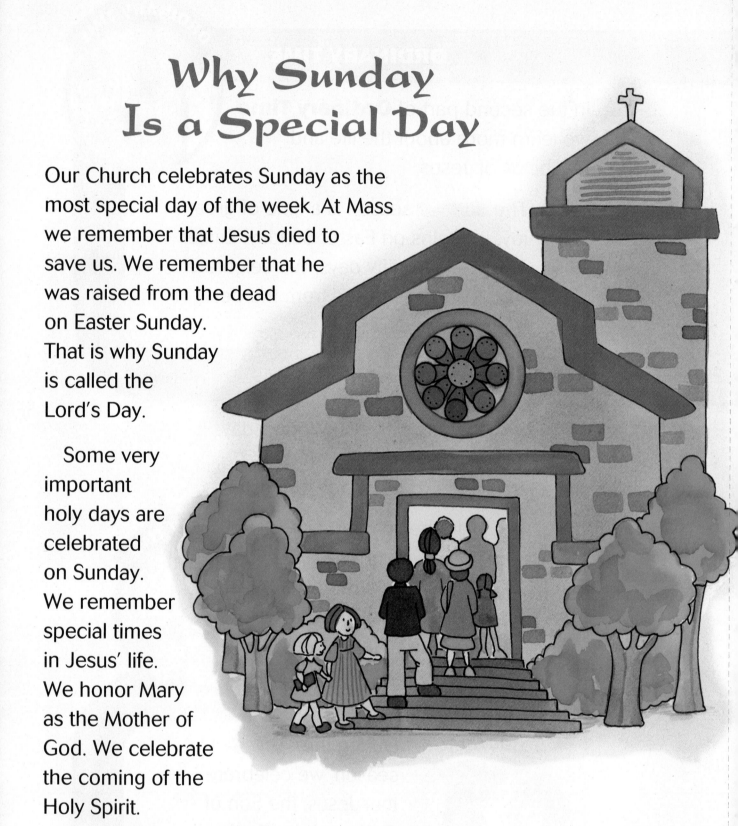

Our Church celebrates Sunday as the most special day of the week. At Mass we remember that Jesus died to save us. We remember that he was raised from the dead on Easter Sunday. That is why Sunday is called the Lord's Day.

Some very important holy days are celebrated on Sunday. We remember special times in Jesus' life. We honor Mary as the Mother of God. We celebrate the coming of the Holy Spirit.

Because Sunday is the Lord's Day, we take time to relax. We spend time with our family and friends. We try to be helpful and kind.

Guardian Angels

I am sending an angel before you to guard you on the way.

Based on Exodus 23:20

People Who Guard Us

Our family cares for us. They try to keep us safe. Sometimes we need other people to guard us and guide us.

Tell about the guards you see.

Activity

Draw how someone who guards you helps to keep you safe.

A Special Gift from God

God gives every person a guardian angel. Guardian angels protect us and guide us. They try to keep us from harm.

You can pray to your guardian angel. You can ask your angel to help you make good choices. You can pray that your angel will help you do what God wants. Pray the prayer to your guardian angel on page 13.

We celebrate the Feast of the Holy Guardian Angels on October 2.

Guardian angel, you are a gift from God. Thank you for watching over me. Amen.

Advent

Make ready the way of the Lord.

Based on Isaiah 40:3

Welcome to Our Home!

Sometimes we welcome guests to our home. We want our guests to be happy. So we get ready to welcome them in special ways. A friendly welcome makes our guests feel special.

Activity

Circle the pictures that show some of the ways your family welcomes guests.

A Time to Get Ready

During **Advent** we get ready to welcome Jesus. We prepare our hearts. We do things for each other to show we care.

These are some of the ways our Church prepares us to welcome Jesus.

Each Sunday we light another candle on the Advent wreath.

We read Bible stories about people who waited for Jesus.

We care for those in need.

Jesus,
help me get ready
to welcome you.
Amen.

Saint Nicholas

Be my follower by helping others.

Based on Matthew 19:21

Sharing

When you were a baby, you did not know how to share. Now you are older. You know it is important to share what you have with others.

Jesus Asks Us to Share

Even when it is hard, Jesus asks us to share what we have with others. Saint Nicholas did what Jesus asks. You may read his story on the next page.

Activity

Draw your favorite toy.

Is it easy to share it with others?
Circle your answer.

Yes   **No**

Bishop Nicholas

When Nicholas grew up, he became a bishop. He saw many poor children and many children without families. He wanted to find ways to share his riches.

At night, when everyone was asleep, Bishop Nicholas went to the homes of poor children. There he left gifts of fruit, candy, and money on their doorsteps. Then he slipped quietly away. He did not want to be noticed!

Bishop Nicholas was a follower of Jesus. Nicholas shared what he had with those who had very little. We celebrate the Feast of Saint Nicholas on December 6.

Saint Nicholas, help us share our things with others. Amen.

Christmas

 I have come from God to bring you good news.

Based on Luke 2:10

A Promise

"Guess what? My big brother promised to play soccer with all of us," said Sammy.

Sammy is very excited. He wants his brother to keep his promise.

Activity

Draw a picture about a promise that you made to someone.

God Keeps a Promise

On **Christmas** we gather at Mass. We listen carefully to the Gospel story.

There were shepherds watching their sheep nearby. An angel sent by God appeared. The angel said, "Do not be afraid. I have come from God to bring you good news. God has kept his promise. Today Jesus has been born. You will find him lying in a manger." The shepherds ran and found Mary and Joseph. They found the Baby Jesus lying in a manger. The shepherds praised God for all they had seen.

Based on Luke 2:8–20

GLORY TO GOD
PEACE ON EARTH

God our Father, thank you for keeping your promise and sending Jesus to be with us. Amen.

The Holy Family

 Happy are you who love God and walk in his ways.

Based on Psalm 128:1

What Does Holy Mean?

Do you know what it means to be holy? To be holy means to be like God.

What is God like?
God is full of love.
God brings peace.
God is kind and gentle.
God cares for us.
God forgives us.

Activity

God has made us to be holy.

Color the words that show what wonderful ways our families can act to be holy.

Jesus' Family

The family of Jesus is called the Holy Family. Mary is Jesus' mother. Joseph is Mary's husband and Jesus' foster father. Jesus loved and obeyed Mary and Joseph. They were kind and caring to Jesus and each other.

Feast of the Holy Family

During Christmas Time, we celebrate the Feast of the Holy Family of Jesus, Mary and Joseph. We celebrate the love that the members of the Holy Family have for each other. We honor God's love for all families.

Holy Family,
help our families
to be more
holy like yours.
Amen.

Mary, the Holy the Mother of God

Hail Mary!
You are full of God's grace.

Based on Luke 1:28

Mary Cares for Jesus

Look carefully at the pictures on this page.
Each picture shows how Mary cared for
her Son, Jesus.

Activity

Circle the picture of Mary caring
for Jesus that you like best.
Tell why you like the picture.

God Chose Mary

God chose Mary to be the Mother of Jesus. We call Mary the Mother of God. Mary is very special.

Mary cared for Jesus. Jesus wants Mary to love and care for us, too. He gave her to us as our special Mother. She loves us and cares for us. Mary prays for us. She prays to her Son, Jesus.

We celebrate the Solemnity of Mary, the Holy Mother of God on January 1.

Mary,
pray for us and
for all children.
Amen.

Lent: Followers of Jesus

Come, follow me!

Based on John 1:43

More like Jesus

Every day we try to do what Jesus would do. To be followers of Jesus, we are called to live as Jesus showed us. We are called to love and care for each other.

Activity

You are a follower of Jesus. Draw yourself in the picture with the other followers of Jesus.

Forty Days

Lent lasts for forty days. During these forty days we get ready to celebrate Easter. We try to remember to become more like Jesus.

What Can We Do?

There are many things we can do during Lent to become more like Jesus. We can do some things with our parish community. We can do other things by ourselves.

With my parish community, I can

 sing at Mass on Sunday.

 care for the sick.

 pray for others.

By myself, I can

 be helpful to my family.

 obey my parents and teachers.

 forgive others.

Jesus, I want to be more like you. Help me to be kind and forgiving. Amen.

Lent: God's Promises

 I came to give you new life that will last forever.

Based on John 10:28

New Life

Jesus promises his followers the gift of new life. At Baptism, we become part of the Church community. The holy water of Baptism is a sign of our new life in Jesus.

Activity

Baptism life new brings

Write a sentence about Baptism with the words on the rainbow. Then color the rainbow.

_____

- - - - - - - - - - - - - - - - - - - -

_____

- - - - - - - - - - - - - - - - - - - -

_____

Noah and the Flood

The Bible tells a story about Noah and a big flood. In the story, God sends water to flood the earth. Rain pours down for forty days. The rain almost washes everything away.

God saves Noah and his family from the flood. When the waters dry up, God makes a promise. God says that he will never let a flood destroy the Earth again. Then God sends a rainbow as a sign of his promise.

Based on Genesis 9:8–15

Loving God, thank you for the gift of Baptism. I promise to follow Jesus always. Amen.

Noah's Ark, 1978, Zeldis, Malcah (b.1931) The Jewish Museum, NY

Holy Week

Blessed is he who comes as our king!

Based on Luke 19:38

Palm Sunday

The first day of Holy Week is called Palm Sunday. It is the Sunday before Easter. We remember how Jesus came into Jerusalem.

Activity

Read the story below.
Use the pictures to help you.

Palms are branches of  .

Palm trees grow in hot, places.

One day a crowd of  cheered and waved palms.

The people were happy to see .

They had a great parade to honor Jesus.

Three Holy Days

Holy Week ends with three holy days. They are Holy Thursday, Good Friday, and Holy Saturday. On these days, we gather at church. We remember how Jesus showed his love for us.

Palm Sunday Mass

At Mass on Palm Sunday, we hold palm branches. We listen to the Gospel story about Jesus going into the city of Jerusalem. We hear how the joyful crowd welcomes Jesus by shouting, "Hosanna!"

We walk into church with the priest and our parish community. Like the people of Jerusalem, we say, "Blessed is he who comes as our king!" (based on Luke 19:38).

After Mass we take our palm branches home. We welcome Jesus into our hearts and homes.

Lord Jesus, we shout "Hosanna!" We welcome you as our King. Amen.

Easter

I have seen the Lord. He is alive!

Based on John 20:18

Signs of Spring

Imagine that it is Sunday afternoon.
You are taking a walk with your family.
The sun is shining. The breeze feels warm.
The air smells fresh and clean. You see
many signs of new life. You
are very happy that
spring is here.

Activity

Look at the picture.
Circle the signs of
new life that you see.

Jesus Is Alive!

Jesus died on a cross. His followers were very sad. They felt scared and all alone. They missed Jesus very much. Three days later God raised Jesus from the dead. God gave Jesus the gift of new life. Jesus' friends were filled with joy. The Risen Jesus was with them again. They thanked God for raising Jesus to new life.

We Celebrate Easter

Easter is our greatest feast. We celebrate Jesus' new life. We believe that we will share new life with Jesus forever. On Easter Sunday we go to Mass. We sing joyful songs. We pray joyful prayers. We say, "Alleluia."

Risen Jesus, help us share in your new life. Alleluia! Amen.

Holy People

Whatever you do to help another person, you do to me.

Based on Matthew 25:40

Helping Others

God made each person special. Jesus tells us to help one another. Children can help in many ways.

Activity

Circle the pictures that show a child helping someone.

Missionaries of Charity

Blessed Mother Teresa spent most of her life helping poor and sick people in India. She saw Christ in each person that she met. Along the way, many women joined her. They became religious sisters called Missionaries of Charity.

Bishops around the world asked these sisters to come to their countries. Now the Missionaries of Charity do their holy work in many places. They bring the love of Christ to each person they meet.

> Jesus, I want to help people. Help me see you in each person that needs my help.
> Amen.

OUR CATHOLIC HERITAGE

WHAT CATHOLICS BELIEVE

We can learn about our faith from the Bible and from the teachings of the Church.

ABOUT
THE BIBLE

The Bible is a special book about God. Some stories in the Bible tell how God loves and cares for people. Other stories tell about Jesus and his followers.

God chose many people to write the Bible. We believe that the Bible is the Word of God.

You can learn more about the Bible on pages 17–21 and in Chapter 3.

ABOUT
THE TRINITY

We believe that there is only one God.
We believe that one God is in Three Persons.
The Three Persons are God the Father,
God the Son, and God the Holy Spirit.
We call the Three Persons the **Holy Trinity**.

We Believe in God the Father

God the Father created the world. He created all of us. Everything God made shows his love.

We are God's children. Like a loving father, God watches over us. He wants us to take care of the world. God wants us to care for each other.

We Believe in God the Son

The Son of God the Father became man. His name is Jesus. He lived on Earth to teach us how to love his Father and one another.

Jesus died on the Cross and rose from the dead. He saved us from sin. Jesus Christ is our Savior.

We Believe in God the Holy Spirit

The Holy Spirit is God. He is the gift of the love of God the Father and God the Son. The Holy Spirit is always with us.

The Holy Spirit gives us grace to help us follow Jesus. Grace is God's loving presence in our lives.

ABOUT
THE CATHOLIC CHURCH

We belong to the Catholic Church. We are called Catholics. We are followers of Jesus.

The pope is the leader of the Catholic Church all over the world. He lives in Rome. We call the pope our Holy Father.

A bishop is the leader of a diocese. A diocese is made up of many parishes. A bishop teaches and cares for the people of his diocese.

A priest serves the people of a parish. He celebrates Mass with the parish community. He teaches people about the Good News of Jesus. A priest needs many helpers to care for all the people in the parish.

ambo

candle →

ABOUT
A VISIT TO CHURCH

A Catholic church is a very special place to visit.

We go to church to worship God. We go to church to celebrate Mass with our parish community.

Look at the picture. It shows some things that we can see in our parish church.

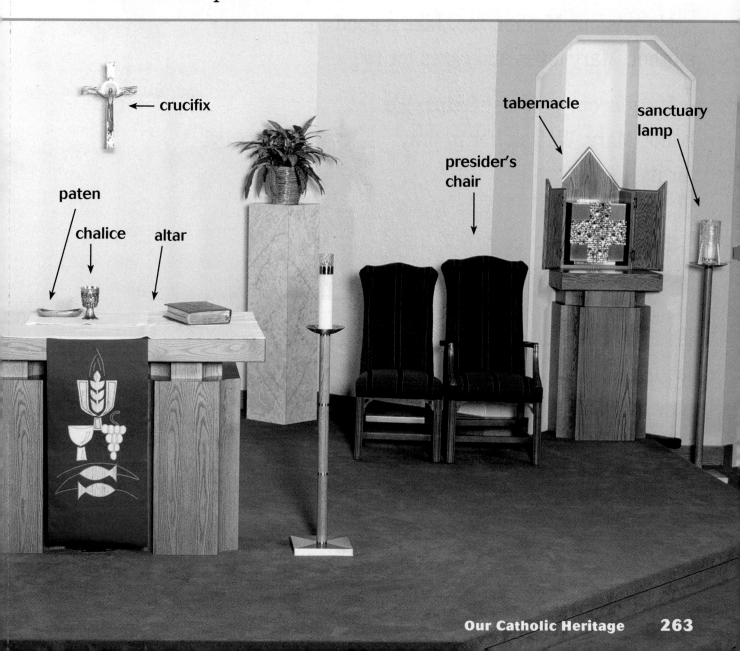

crucifix

tabernacle

sanctuary lamp

presider's chair

paten

chalice

altar

ABOUT
MARY

Mary was good and holy. God chose Mary to be the mother of his Son, Jesus.

Mary loved and trusted God. She loved and cared for Jesus.

Mary is our Mother, too. Like a good mother, Mary loves and cares for us.

Mary is our greatest **Saint**. We honor Mary. We ask her to pray for us.

ABOUT
NEW LIFE FOREVER

Jesus teaches us how to love God and others. Jesus says that if we act with love, we will have new life. Jesus promises that if we love God and others, we will live forever.

When we die, we will be with Jesus, Mary, and all the good and holy people who ever lived. Happiness with God forever is called Heaven.

HOW CATHOLICS WORSHIP

Worship is giving honor and praise to God. We worship when we pray and when we celebrate the Sacraments.

ABOUT THE SACRAMENTS

The Sacraments are celebrations of God's love for us. We celebrate that we are followers of Jesus Christ. We celebrate that we share in his new life.

Baptism is the Sacrament of welcome into the Church. At Baptism, we become children of God. The water of Baptism washes away all sin and fills us with God's grace.

Confirmation is the Sacrament in which the Holy Spirit makes our faith in Christ stronger. The Holy Spirit helps us share the Good News of Jesus.

Eucharist is the Sacrament in which Jesus Christ shares himself with us. We receive the Body and Blood of Christ.

Penance and Reconciliation is the Sacrament of forgiveness. We say that we are sorry for our sins. We celebrate God's forgiveness.

Anointing of the Sick is the Sacrament that brings the peace of Jesus to people who are sick.

Holy Orders is the Sacrament that celebrates the mission of deacons, priests, and bishops. These men are called to serve God's people in a special way.

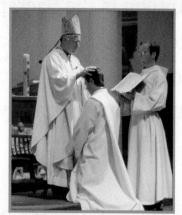

Matrimony is the Sacrament that celebrates the love of a man and a woman for each other. They promise to be faithful. They are ready to begin their family life.

ABOUT THE MASS

1. Our celebration begins. The priest and other ministers go to the altar. We stand and sing a welcome song.

2. We make the Sign of the Cross. The priest welcomes us with these words: "The Lord be with you."

3. We remember our sins. We ask God to forgive us.

4. We listen to the Word of God in readings from the Bible. After each of the first two readings we say, "Thanks be to God."

5. The priest or deacon reads the Gospel story. The word "gospel" means "good news." We stand and listen to the Good News story of Jesus. We say, "Praise to you, Lord Jesus Christ."

6. The priest or deacon helps us understand Jesus' message in a special talk called the homily.

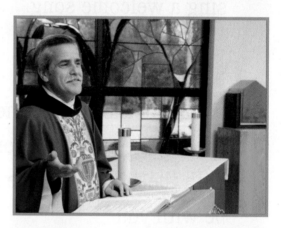

7. In the Prayer of the Faithful, we ask God to help the Church, our country, and all of God's people.

8. We bring the gifts of bread and wine to the altar for the special meal with Jesus. We remember that Jesus always loves us.

9. The priest blesses God and offers him our gifts of bread and wine. We say, "Blessed be God for ever."

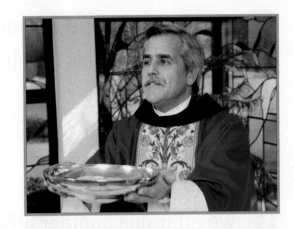

10. We thank and praise God for all of our blessings. We especially thank God for the gift of Jesus.

11. The priest prays as Jesus did at the Last Supper. Our gifts of bread and wine become the Body and Blood of Jesus Christ.

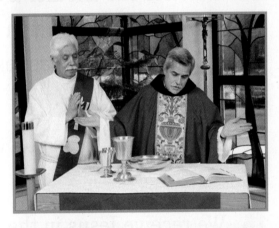

12. The priest holds up the Body and Blood of Jesus. He says a prayer to praise God. We answer, "Amen."

13. We say the Lord's Prayer. This is the prayer that Jesus taught us to say.

14. We offer one another a Sign of Peace. This is a sign that reminds us to live as Jesus teaches us to live.

15. We receive Jesus in the Eucharist. Sharing Jesus' Body and Blood in a special way means that we are promising to follow Jesus.

16. We receive God's blessing. We answer, "Amen." We sing a song of praise. We go in peace to love and serve God and one another.

HOW CATHOLICS LIVE

Jesus teaches us how to live. He gives us the Holy Spirit and the Church to help us.

ABOUT
THE GREAT COMMANDMENT

God's laws are really one Great Commandment. Jesus said, "You must love God above all things and love your neighbor as yourself" (based on Mark 12:30–31). The Great Commandment tells us how to love God and other people.

ABOUT
THE NEW COMMANDMENT

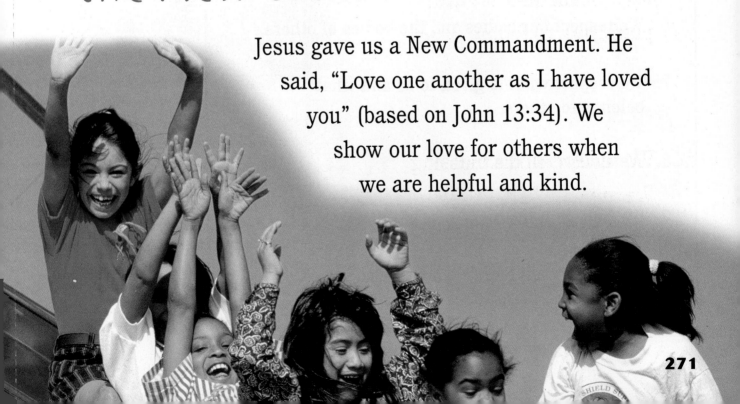

Jesus gave us a New Commandment. He said, "Love one another as I have loved you" (based on John 13:34). We show our love for others when we are helpful and kind.

ABOUT
THE TEN COMMANDMENTS

We Live God's Law

We show our love for God.

1. We believe in God and love God.

2. We use God's name with love.

3. We pray with our parish community at Mass. We keep the Lord's Day holy.

We show our love for our neighbor.

4. We obey our parents and those who care for us.

5. We care for all living things.

6. We respect our bodies and the bodies of others.

7. We respect what is given to us and what belongs to others.

8. We always tell the truth.

9. We rejoice in the happiness of others.

10. We do not want more than we need.

ABOUT
SIN AND FORGIVENESS

Sin is a choice to do something that we know is wrong. Sin is turning away from God. Sin hurts our friendship with people.

We know that God loves us. We know that he is always ready to forgive us. God wants us to be sorry for our sins. He wants us to promise to do better. We can ask the Holy Spirit to help us.

✝ Dear God,
I am sorry for what I did wrong. I will try to do better. I will love and care for others. Please send the Holy Spirit to help me. Amen.

Jesus teaches us to love and care for others. Sometimes people do wrong things to us. We should always be ready to forgive them. We can say, "I forgive you."

ABOUT VOCATIONS

We become members of the Catholic Church at Baptism. God calls us to love him and serve him in a special way. This is called our vocation.

Religious Vocations

God calls some people to a special life of service in the Church. The call to be a priest, deacon, and religious sister or brother is called a religious vocation.

Many priests serve the Church by being leaders of parish communities. Others teach or work with poor people.

Deacons help the priests in parishes. They lead celebrations of Baptism and marriage. At Mass, they teach people about the Bible readings. Deacons visit the sick and pray with families of people who have died.

Let us pray that more men and women will answer God's call to a religious vocation.

Many religious sisters and brothers serve in parishes. Some work in schools and hospitals. Others share the Good News of Jesus with poor people all over the world.

Other Calls to Serve

God calls all Catholics to serve the Church. Some Catholics help at Mass. They welcome the people. They read aloud from the Bible. They lead the singing of holy songs. They help give communion to the people.

Other Catholics teach children and adults about God's love. They share the Good News about Jesus. They teach people to pray in different ways.

Many Catholics visit the sick and help the poor. They give money to help people in need.

As you grow up, God will call you to serve the Church in special ways. Will you be ready to say yes to his call?

HOW CATHOLICS PRAY

Prayer is talking and listening to God. We can pray anywhere and at any time. God is everywhere. God always hears our prayers.

ABOUT KINDS OF PRAYER

There are many different ways to pray. We can say the prayers we learn at home and in church. We can use our own words to pray, too. Sometimes we can just be quiet in God's presence. We do not even have to say any words.

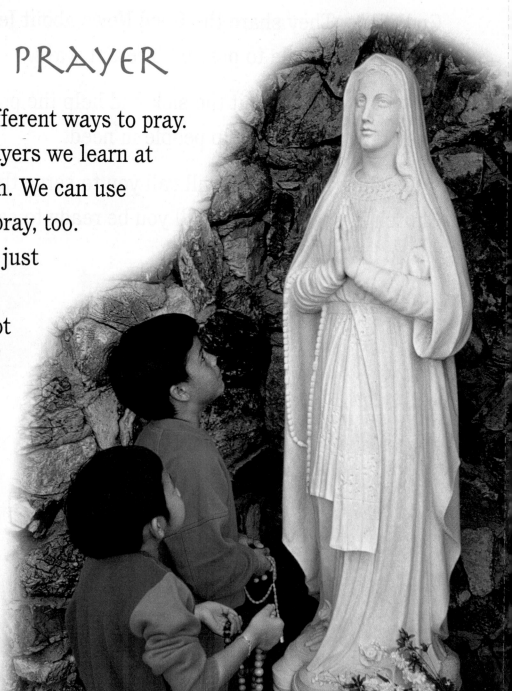

The children are praying the Rosary to honor Mary.

Our thoughts can be a prayer. Our hopes can be a prayer. This kind of prayer is called meditation. In meditation we use our imagination to think about God. We think about what God wants us to do.

We can use our bodies when we pray. When we make the Sign of the Cross, we use our hands. Sometimes we kneel when we pray. We can even sing or dance as a prayer to God.

We are never alone when we pray. God hears our prayers.

ABOUT
THE LORD'S PRAYER

The Lord's Prayer is a very special prayer.
Jesus taught us the words. In this prayer,
Jesus teaches us to call God "Our Father." We
believe that God is everyone's loving Father.

Our Father, who art in heaven, hallowed be thy name;
> God is our Father. We praise God's holy name.

thy kingdom come,
> We pray that everyone will know God's love and live
> in peace.

thy will be done on earth as it is in heaven.
> We pray that everyone will follow God's Law.

Give us this day our daily bread,
> We pray for our needs and the needs of others.

and forgive us our trespasses, as we forgive
those who trespass against us;
> We ask God to forgive us when we sin.
> We remember that we must forgive others.

and lead us not into temptation
> We ask God to help us make good choices.

but deliver us from evil.
> We pray that God will protect us from harm.

Amen.
> "Amen" means that we believe the words we say.

Write-in Glossary

adore
(page 126)

_____

- - - - - - - - - - - - - - - -

To _____ Jesus Christ means "to worship or honor him as the Son of God."

Advent
(page 240)

_____

- - - - - - - - - - - - - - - - - - - -

_____ is the time before Christmas when we get ready to welcome Jesus into our lives.

Amen
(page 197)

_____

- - - - - - - - - - - - - - -

_____ means "Yes, I believe. It is true." We often say "Amen" at the end of prayers.

angel
(pages 113, 238)

_____

- -

An _____ is a helper or a messenger from God. Guardian angels protect and guide us.

Anointing of the Sick
(page 266)

_____   _____

- - - - - - - - - - - - - - - - - - -   - - - - - - - - - -

_____ of the _____ is a Sacrament that brings the peace of Christ to people who are sick.

Baptism
(page 81)

_____

- -

_____ is a celebration of welcome into the Catholic community.

Bible
(page 49)

_____

- - - - - - - - - - - - - - - - - - - -

The _____ is the written Word of God. God chose special people to write the Bible.

Blessed Sacrament
(page 124)

The _____ is another name for the Eucharist.

blessing
(page 42)

A _____ is a gift from God. It can also be a prayer that asks for God's protection and care.

Catholic Church
(page 29)

The _____ is the community of Jesus' followers to which we belong.

Christ
(page 123)

_____ is another name for Jesus. It tells us that he was sent by God to save all people.

Christians
(page 175)

_____ are people who love Jesus Christ and follow him.

Christmas
(page 244)

_____ is the time when we celebrate the birth of Jesus.

church
(page 38)

A _____ is a special place where Catholics come together to pray.